ANALYZING & INTERPRETING
LITERATURE

CLEP* Study Guide

© 2014 Breely Crush Publishing, LLC

*CLEP is a registered trademark of the College Entrance Examination Board which does not endorse this book.

971082413143

Published by Breely Crush Publishing, LLC
10808 River Front Parkway
South Jordan, UT 84095
www.breelycrushpublishing.com

ISBN-10: 1-61433-002-6
ISBN-13: 978-1-61433-002-8

Printed and bound in the United States of America.

*CLEP is a registered trademark of the College Entrance Examination Board which does not endorse this book.

Table of Contents

Interpreting Literature

Like most things in life worth pursuing, the more effort we put into the study of literature, the more it gives back to us. It becomes easier and more enjoyable to read and appreciate great works of literary art. Our lives become richer and fuller because of our experience.

Many classic works of literature can be challenging, especially for today's students. Many great works were 17 written years ago when the English language was quite different from what it is today. Shakespeare's works certainly comes to mind. Some writers are simply more challenging than others are. A writer like Edgar Alan Poe, for example has written dozens of superbly crafted short stories and poems – and nearly all are readily accessible to modern readers. On the other hand, modern writers like William Faulkner and Virginia Wolf – with their intricate, complex thought and prose – take greater effort to appreciate.

Interpreting literature has another unique characteristic: two people can read the same story, poem, or play and end up with quite different interpretations. That is to be expected. The reason is simple: a relationship exists between the reader and writer. While the writer attempts to communicate something in a unique way, the reader also has a job to do – i.e. interpretation. If you have ever played the game in which two people are given identical information and then had to repeat back what they heard with very different results, you know that we understand and interpret what we see and hear in very different ways. Our comprehension shaped by our own personalities, education, experience, and culture. From a communications standpoint, the process is called encoding and decoding. The author encodes certain messages and we decode them. The quality of this process depends on a shared language and experience to be successful. So, even reading the same story – the same words on the page or action on the stage – we are not always in agreement about what has taken place. So does that mean that literature is a like a Rorschach test with words in which there is no truth of a story – that anything goes?

That would be an extreme position to take. What we do expect – quite fairly, it would seem – is that personal interpretations of a story are permitted as long as the student supports his or her viewpoint with specific details from the story itself. In other words, our job is not to create a new story to support our point of view, but to use what the author has actually created as the foundation of our interpretation.

How to Read Literary Works

Start by reading the story straight through just as you would any other story you looked forward to reading. Keep in mind that most authors are not writing for English professors or literary critics. Mostly they write for real people like you whom they hope will enjoy and appreciate the story on its own terms. Keep your analytical reader under wraps at the outset.

Go through the story a second time. Is there anything that seems extraordinary to you – vivid scenes, important characters, moments where the author has made an extra effort to describe a place or event? What clues does the writer leave behind about the real reasons he wrote this story? What is his purpose? Which themes are in his work?

After the second reading, make quick, informal notes about the story as you see it: what the story is about, the character profiles, key scenes that you remember, the themes and story settings that stand out for you.

Literary Criticism

As you research various stories, poems, and plays, you will likely find essays and other critical works written by people who have spent their professional lives reading, interpreting, and illuminating literary works. Many are college and university teachers, but some are freelance writers and journalists who specialize in literary criticism. They frequently specialize in certain types of literature: novels, plays, poetry, and often within certain time periods and languages.

So how can these critics of literature help you? Most have written extensively about their areas of expertise. You can find copies of their essays and books in most libraries. How they interpret the literary works you read can provide a helpful starting point for your own analysis. The important thing to keep in mind is that while helpful – these critics often have biases and blind spots of their own. Many times, they belong to groups of critics who share the same biases and approaches.

OK, so what are some of the key terms we need to know for fictional stories?

Fiction: Any story that is written in which the characters are not real. This refers to both short stories and longer forms such as the novel.

Tale: Similar in meaning to "fiction;" sometimes described as "telling a tale."

Short Story: This is brief, prose fiction that is usually about only one character and situation.

Parable: This a short story with a moral. The Bible contains many famed parable stories.

Allegory: Where abstract ideas are represented by characters or other means.

Rectitude: Morally correct or upright.

Fable: Similar to a parable, a fable is a brief story that points to a moral. It usually has animals that talk.

Initiation Story: a story where the main character goes through "rites of initiation" such as getting a driver's license, first date, getting married, etc.

Young Goodman Brown

Go online and read the story of "Young Goodman Brown" at http://www.online-literature.com/hawthorne/158/

Which of these previous definitions describe the story of Young Goodman Brown? What was that story even about? Do you see any deep parallels or representations of something else? This is how the literature on the CLEP test will be. You will have to sometimes re-read passages to get the full meaning. Now re-read the story with those above terms in mind. See if you can discuss and understand the following discussion questions. This is for your own understanding. If you want to go back to the web page and do a search for a particular word or passage, hit CTRL and F at the same time, then type the word you are searching for in the dialog box. Rolf M. Gunnar created these discussion questions.

1. How does the setting add to the meaning of the story: sunset and night, dreary road, gloomiest trees, narrow path creeping through, lonely, peculiarity in solitude?

2. Discuss the significance of "Faith kept me back awhile" (55).

3. Why do you think Faith wore *pink* ribbons? Hint: think of Hawthorne's novel, *The Scarlet Letter* and the connotations of colors.

4. Discuss the significance of the second traveler (sic.), " . . . apparently in the same rank of life as Goodman Brown and bearing a considerable resemblance to him, though perhaps more in expression than features. Still they might have been taken for father and son" (55).

5. Interpret the description of the staff "which bore the likeness of a great black snake, so curiously wrought that it might almost be seen to twist and wriggle like a living serpent. This, of course, must have been an ocular deception, assisted by the uncertain light." Why the uncertainty?

6. When the fellow traveler states, "I have been well acquainted with your family... I helped your grandfather, the constable, when he lashed the Quaker woman so smartly through the streets of Salem. ... The deacons of many a church have drunk wine with me; the select men of divers town make me their chairman; and a majority of the Great and General Court are firm believers of my interest"(56), what do we begin to understand about him? Though this character, what is Hawthorne telling us about evil?

7. Interpret: "...don't kill me with laughing" (57).

8. Discuss the meaning of the encounter with Goody Cloyse. "... and in the very image of my old gossip, Goodman Brown, the grandfather of the silly fellow that now is"(58).

9. After Goodman Brown refuses to go any farther and the traveler throws him the maple stick and leaves, discuss Goodman Brown's attitude and conscience.

10. After the minister and Deacon Gookin ride by, what happens to Goodman Brown? Why is this significant? Discuss the statement: "With heaven above and Faith below, I will yet stand firm against the devil!"

11. What does the black mass of cloud symbolize - the confused and doubtful sound of voices?

12. Discuss the meaning(s): "My Faith is gone!"(62).

13. Describe what Goodman Brown saw when he arrived at the meeting - the grave, reputable, and pious people, the chaste dames and dewy virgins, the revered pastor, and that the good "shrank not from the wicked." Discuss the meaning.

14. The dark figure states, "Welcome, my children, to the communion of your race. Ye have found thus young your nature and your destiny" (65). Discuss.

15. How does Goodman Brown treat people the next day? What happens to him? Why?

16. Is this story about an inward psychological journey where Goodman Brown discovers evil in himself but refuses to acknowledge it? Defend your answer.

17. Is this story a criticism of the village's hypocrisy? Defend your answer.

18. "Young Goodman Brown" is a moral allegory. An allegory can be defined as an extended metaphor - using one thing to represent another - a story with dual meanings. There is a surface or literal meaning as well as a secondary meaning. In other words, Hawthorne uses his story to reveal a moral lesson or lessons. Discuss the moral lesson(s) you find that the story reveals.

19. In allegories characters are usually personifications of abstract qualities. For example, a character can represent a human trait or behavior. With that in mind, discuss the significance of the names "Young Goodman Brown" and "Faith."

If you can answer all of these questions, having read the story two or three times, you are doing great. A good portion of the passages on the test will be dealing with "difficult" passages and analyzing them and this is great experience.

 # Plot and "Story of an Hour"

To prepare for a discussion of plot, read the "Story of an Hour" by Kate Chopin at http://www.vcu.edu/engweb/webtexts/hour/.

What is plot? Stated simply, a plot is a series of events – things that happen – that carry a story from beginning to end. In some stories – "The Adventures of Huckleberry Finn," for example – the plot unfolds at a fast and furious pace. In other stories, "The Scarlet Letter," for example, relatively few events actually take place. Most of the story happens in the minds and dialogue of the characters.

People read and enjoy stories for different reasons. For some it is the plot itself – they are excited and captivated by what happens. They want to know what happens next. Often, the "what happens next?" question provides the motivation we need to keep reading. We want to know how the story ends.

Usually plots move sequentially from the chronological beginning to the middle to the end. Real life follows that pattern (for most of us) and art, in this case, mirrors life. However, for a variety of reasons, authors often move back and forth in time. The story might start in the present – e.g. our main character opens the story sitting in a wheelchair – but then at some point the author moves the plot back in time to explain why or how the character ended up in that wheelchair. Somewhat rarer, an author moves the plot into the future to show what will happen, then uses the story to explain how the future unfolds.

When a writer sits down to write a short story, novel, play, even a poem, the writer inevitably starts with a blank piece of paper – in modern times an empty computer screen. With the first word written the writer is making a choice. The same for the second word, and the word after that. And so on. Creative writing is all about making choices. That is important to know. It should lead you to ask questions like these: why this word and not another, why start here and not there, why in this place, this season, this historical place? Some choices are what we call "happy accidents." It could be the series of words, the juxtaposition of scenes or characters. Such moments are certainly joyful ones for the writer, and if they make sense in the context of the rest of the story, those accidents survive in the finished manuscript. More frequently, the writer is making a series of well-considered choices. It is our examination into the reasons behind those choices that makes our study of literature so much fun. . . and a challenge!

When a writer starts a story in the middle of the plot, we refer to that as **in medias res**. If the writer makes the story go back in time, we call it a **flashback**.

Is a story simply a series of events that take place – the plot? No. A story is more than just the sum of its events. It is *about* something. So, one of the questions you want to ask is: "What is this story really about?" To answer with a summary of the plot is clearly missing the point.

Take Melville's "Moby Dick" for example. As we can see in our own summary of the events in the novel, a great deal of action takes place. There are the encounters with other whaling ships, life-threatening battles with whales, the dangerous storms that Ahab and his crew survive on the Pequod. Is that what the story is about? Is it "Vengeful whaling captain risks his and his crew's life to kill Moby Dick?" While that might be closer to what Melville had in mind, it still falls short of a complete answer to the question: What is the story, "Moby Dick," *really* about? For the answer, we have to look at other elements in addition to the plot. What are the main themes? What symbols are used? What transformations take place in the main characters?

Another example: "The Necklace" by Guy de Maupassant appears to be a story about a woman who borrows a friend's diamond necklace to wear to a fancy ball; she loses the necklace and then spends years trying to pay off the cost of replacing it. That's what happens – it's a summary of the events, the plot. After you read this short but deftly written story, what would you say it is about?

"What is this story about?" means going beyond mere events. Another way to approach this question is to think about the motives of the writer in creating the story. One could argue, for example, that Melville simply wanted to tell an exciting whaling story – which is clearly an element of "Moby Dick." However, as readers we are given numerous clues that Melville had a greater purpose than that.

Setting

Ask yourself: where are we physically? What time is it? – the hour, day, time of year – but also the season and the historical context of the story. Story and setting are inextricably bound. The main character exists somewhere, in some time. Could a story like "Moby Dick" possibly exist outside a world of vast oceans and creaking whaling ships? Imagine "The Scarlet Letter" removed from the austere world of Puritan New England. Both seem impossible to imagine. Sometimes setting is chosen as a way to create a certain mood or atmosphere – the stuffy office where Bartleby the Scrivener plies his trade creates the sense of futility that Melville needed to make his story work.

Often the setting acts like another character in the story and has an effect on the plot and the other characters. For example, the austere Puritan setting of "The Scarlet Letter" affects the behavior of Hester and the other main characters. Setting can also be symbolic. In Hawthorne's brooding short story, "Young Goodman Brown," the setting of the forest on the outskirts of town represents the antithesis of the ordered, morally constrained society of the Puritan village.

Setting and time frequently provide the moral or social context that makes the plot and characters credible; setting both influences and explains their behavior. Imagine a fictional character that travels from a quiet small town in rural Georgia to the garish, exciting world of casinos and endless nightlife in Las Vegas. It is not hard to imagine how the setting might influence the character's behavior.

Recognizing that the author is consciously crafting a setting for the story, ask yourself: what is his intention in creating this particular setting? Does it have a purpose other than as a backdrop for the plot and characters? What influence does the setting have on the characters? On advancing the plot? Does it have any thematic or symbolic purpose in the story? Finally, pay attention to how the author paints this backdrop of time and place. Is it a long, elaborately painted setting, or does the author do it in a few short, simple brush strokes, leaving the rest to our imagination? In the opening to "The Last of the Mohicans," James Fenimore Cooper opens his novel with a lengthy description of the historical context of the story – the French and Indian Wars that took place in Colonial America during the late 1750s.

The short story, "The Yellow Wallpaper," takes place at the turn of the century. Would it be the same story or very different if it took place in the present time? The author set the story in the nursery. Is there a special reason for that choice? In "The Storm," the story quite logically happens during a storm. How is that significant? Would it have been the same story if it took place on a pleasant day?

The setting of a story can tell us a great deal about the story's themes. It also frequently provides insight into the characters and how they behave.

Epiphany is when a character has a sudden realization. An example would be a wife who suddenly puts together all the clues about her husband and realizes he is having an affair. Also referred to as "like being struck by lighting."

Exposition is where we meet the characters and the setting.

Rising action is where we find out about the conflict and includes all new problems we learn about along the way.

Falling action, resolution and **denouement** are all the same thing. It is what happens after the climax and lets the writers show us what happens in the end. You might remember at the end of some movies, we get to see all the characters and where they ended up. This is a great example of denouement.

Here is a simple outline for a basic short story:

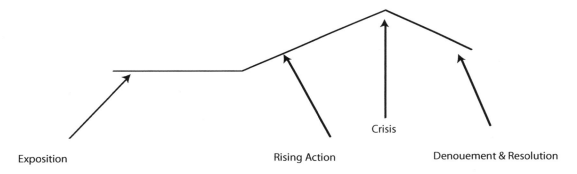

Exposition   Rising Action   Crisis   Denouement & Resolution

- Based on Story of an Hour, what would be the exposition?
- What would be the rising action?
- What is the crisis?
- What is the resolution?
- Does it have a happy ending? Do stories have to?

When you read a story or a piece of poetry, ask yourself, what did the author want to get across with this piece? What the purpose to entertain, inform, persuade or describe?

In creating a story, an author usually tries to arrange the sequence of events – the elements of the plot – in a way that creates tension, suspense, or heightened interest. Part of the art of literature is knowing how to create that tension or heightened interest. There is usually some crisis or problem that the main character needs to solve. It is the journey towards solving the crisis that often determines the sequence of events and the events themselves. We must be careful to understand that in literature crisis does not always mean a physical crisis, e.g. the protagonist is trapped inside a burning building and cannot find a way out. Often the crisis that motivates the character and suggests the events within the story is a psychological, emotional, or moral crisis. In "The Scarlet Letter," for example, would you classify the crisis faced by Hester's lover, Dimmesdale, as a psychological or moral crisis? Both?

As we mentioned previously, creating literature is about making choices – and that includes the sequence of events in the story. Ask yourself: Why did the author choose to begin the story with this event? Why choose to end it with that event? What has changed between the beginning and the end? Pay special attention to the conflicts that take place: are they inner conflicts, conflicts between the characters, or a conflict within the setting of the story?

You might also consider how the characters change as the story progresses. In F. Scott Fitzgerald's novel, "The Great Gatsby," the main character and narrator, Nick Carraway, arrives on Long Island, a recent Yale graduate from the Midwest. It is 1922 and he has gone east feeling restless but full of hope for the future. After spending the summer with Jay Gatsby and his circle of friends, what changes take place in Nick's views about life and the American dream of material success and social status?

The repetition of events and details often provide an important insight into the purpose of the story – an answer to the question: "what is this story about?" Why, for example, does the narrator of Edgar Allan Poe's "The Tell-tale Heart" repeat himself? Through repetition, we begin to understand what the author thinks is important for us to know. The repetition is there for a purpose. It is a technique used to emphasize an idea, mood, symbol, or theme. Repetition can help lead you to the story's symbolism and theme. Keep in mind, as well, that repetition does not always mean using the exact same word or image. For example, Poe might use the words "gloomy," "darkness," "sepulchral," or – one of his favorite words – "lugubrious" to reinforce the same image for the reader.

Characters

Characters are frequently classified according to the roles they play in a story. Some of the major categories of character include:

- **Protagonist:** This is the main character of the story.

- **Antagonist:** The character who opposes or tries to stop the protagonist from solving the story's crisis.

- **Anti-hero:** A protagonist that does not have what it takes to make him a hero. He is lacking in some way.

- **Major Character:** This character is the protagonist of the story and is the story's focus.

- **Minor Character:** This character plays a supporting role in the story.

- **Flat Character:** This is someone who seems only "sketched in" by the author. We do not know very much about this character.

- **Round Character:** This is a fully developed character. The author tells us both good and bad things about them.

By now, you have probably noticed that some characters are more vivid than others are. With some, you can almost smell the perfume in their hair and see the shine on their shoes. Others are vague figures that drift faceless through the story. This disparity in the depth of characters is sometimes deliberate and sometimes accidental. Writers who are especially talented at creating vivid, multi-dimensional characters might do so for the main and some secondary characters but leave others less well defined. That again is a choice made by the author. Some authors – even some great authors – are less talented at creating character and instead are masters at inventing entertaining plots or elaborate settings. As you will see, characters can be individuals, with unique characteristics, habits, quirks, and personalities, so that they seem like real people; or they can be "types"–that is, they can typify or represent something larger than themselves. Some authors whose main interest is to illuminate an idea or theme might create characters that are more like types than real people.

As noted above, the protagonist's opponent is called the "antagonist." Usually that is another person, but it can be an animal like Moby Dick, or a spirit, or even a natural force like a great storm. Some might argue that it can even be a flaw or trait in the protagonist. Consider "The Great Gatsby," for example. The protagonist is Nick Carraway. Who is the antagonist in Fitzgerald's novel? Is it Gatsby himself? Tom Buchanan? Or is it the illusion of the American dream of materialistic success?

Characters play different roles in a story. Some, are protagonists, others can be antagonists. One question you might ask is this: who or what is preventing the protagonist from reaching a goal, surmounting a crisis, or solving a problem? The answer usually reveals the story's antagonist.

You will also notice that "flat" characters might play an important role in a story but do not change or grow very much. Major or round characters do change or grow. In "The Great Gatsby," Nick's brother-in-law, Tom Buchanan, plays an important role in advancing the plot; after all, it is he who confronted Gatsby and forced his wife, Daisy to drive home with Gatsby. However, unlike Nick, who undergoes a significant personal transformation, Tom remains essentially unchanged as a character.

The names the author selects for the characters can be very helpful in deciding what role they play in the story. Sometimes, the meaning of the name is subtle. In "Moby Dick," the doomed captain is named Ahab, after a Biblical tyrant who came to a bad end. In "The Scarlet Letter," the evil-minded husband who seeks to punish the Reverend Dimmesdale is appropriately named Chillingworth.

Points of View

Read the following stories:
"Gimpel the Fool" at http://salvoblue.homestead.com/gimpel.html
"A Rose for Emily" at http://xroads.virginia.edu/~drbr/wf_rose.html
"Araby" at http://www.bibliomania.com/0/0/29/63/11254/1/frameset.html

Style is the way a story or book is written which shows the author's personal flair and touch. Some different examples of style would be monologue (one person talking to herself or the audience), diary format, etc. Contrast the clipped, sparse style of most of Ernest Hemmingway's stories with the elegant, poetic style of the English writer, Virginia Woolf.

Tone is the mood of a subject, subdued, joyful, explosive, etc. For example, the mood in many of Nathaniel Hawthorne's stories would be described as grim, somber, and dark.

First Person is where the speaker is talking about himself or herself. There may be phrases such as, "I love going to the park. We're going there today."

Stream-of-consciousness is an unedited view of the speaker's (or main character's) mind. Something that flows freely. An example would be:

> It came quicker and quicker. I didn't know she could move so fast. Did she see me move behind this pillar?
> "Carrie," she knifed in. She was right behind me! I turn.
> "Yes?"
> "You forgot your keys."

A **Narrator** is just someone telling the story. They are a participant and may be the main character, as is Nick in "The Great Gatsby."

A **Naïve Narrator** is a narrator that does not understand the conflicts or complications about the story he is telling. But the reader may see through foreshadowing, that two people are about to hit together like a train wreck. A good example is knowing a bank robber is going to rob the Main Street Bank at 8am, a good hour before they open and also that the manager is going to start, as of today, giving the town better service by opening an hour early. The narrator knows both of these items but does not draw the conclusion that things will not go as planned.

Third Person Narrator is not a participant in the story. He reports events such as "she cried all night."

Third Person Objective Narrator is the type of narrator that cannot tell us about any of the thoughts of the characters, but only what they are doing.

Third Person Limited Narrator is the type of narrator that knows all about one character, including their thoughts, but that's all.

Third Person Omniscient Narrator is all knowing. They might have information that the main characters do not have. An example would be, the narrator knows that the main character Jillane is pregnant. Jillane does not know she is and her husband suspects it based on her moods. This narrator also knows other characters thoughts.

Unreliable Narrator is a narrator that is mentally unstable or deranged. For an example, read The Yellow Wallpaper at: http://www.eastoftheweb.com/short-stories/UBooks/YelWal.shtml

Point of View is the way a story is told and by whom.

Style, Tone and Language

The "tone" of a story or novel is the manner of expression the author uses to tell the story. As such, tone represents the author's attitude towards the story and its characters. It is revealed through the word choice and pace of the story. For example, the tone of a story can be suspenseful, sarcastic, witty, thoughtful, poetic, or philosophic. We usually can tell what the tone of the story is from the very beginning of the story. Keep in mind that the tone or attitude of the narrator is not always the same as the author's.

The author's decisions about which words to use and the story's details can tell us a great deal about the tone. Consider, for example, the opening paragraph of "The Adventures of Huckleberry Finn." The narrator is none other than Huck himself. In a brief opening paragraph, he tells us a great deal about himself, the type of informal story we are about to read, and the tone the author, Mark Twain intends to use in telling this story:

> You don't know about me without you have read a book by the name of *The Adventures of Tom Sawyer;* but that ain't no matter. That book was made by Mr. Mark Twain, and he told the truth, mainly. There was things which he stretched, but mainly he told the truth. That is nothing. I never seen anybody but lied one time or another, without it was Aunt Polly, or the widow, or maybe Mary. Aunt Polly – Tom's Aunt Polly, she is – and Mary, and the Widow Douglas is all told about in that book, which is mostly a true book, with some stretchers, as I said before.

That brief passage and its structure and work choice tells us much about Huck, his level of education, his values – especially about lying, and his attitude towards himself and some of the main characters in his life, including the author Mark Twain. The passage also suggests that we might be in store for a few "stretchers" in this story.

Style

Every author seeks to develop a unique writing style – a way of using language and details to express ideas. Style can also tell us much about the story's theme. Mark Twain, in "The Adventures of Huckleberry Finn," uses a colloquial, almost breathless style to represent Huck Finn's youthful exuberance. Twain's language flows like the meandering Mississippi River itself. Consider this excerpt:

So the king sneaked into the wigwam, and took to his bottle for comfort; and before long the duke tackled *his* bottle; and so in about a half an hour they was as thick as thieves again, and the tighter they got, the lovinger they got; and went off a-snoring in each other's arms.

The deliberate, grammatical mistakes – even the occasional made up words like "lovinger" – help define Huck's personality. The flowing style adds to the fast-paced movement of the plot.

William Faulkner presents the theme of isolation in "A Rose for Emily." He highlights Emily's alienation by describing a sense of abundance from which she is excluded. As in many of Faulkner's stories, his sentences are long and seem as lazy as a summer day in the South, a perfect reflection of life in Emily's town. In this story, as in most, Faulkner uses tone and style together to create a mood and theme.

Symbols

As Sigmund Freud, the founder of psychoanalysis once said: "Sometimes a cigar is just a cigar." What he meant is that not everything has dramatic or psychological significance. In literature, too, sometimes a thing is just a thing. In an attempt to understand a story and its themes, we sometimes attach meaning to things that go beyond what they really are. With that caution in mind, let us look at symbolism as a literary device.

A "symbol" is something that suggests more than its literal meaning. What a symbol suggests is frequently determined by the personality and culture of the reader doing the interpretation. For most people, a rose usually stands for love; a skull and crossbones stands for poison. In some societies and cultures, it is possible for those symbols to have other meanings.

Depending on the author, a symbol might have more than one meaning, or the meaning is ambiguous and therefore subject to different interpretations. They suggest or hint, or draw attention to an idea.

In Herman Melville's novel, "Moby Dick," the great white whale has been interpreted in many ways by literary critics. For some, the whale is symbolic of a chaotic, meaningless universe, for others it represents humanity's quest for domination of his environment; for others, the whale is a metaphysical symbol of evil. Which is the correct interpretation? How would you characterize the whale's symbolism? Has Melville deliberately made the interpretation of Moby Dick ambiguous?

Consider "Young Goodman Brown," a short story written by Hawthorne during the same general period as "Moby Dick." As a story about the Puritan conversion experience, many of its symbols seem obvious. Even the names of the main characters, such as "Goodman" and his wife, "Faith," resonate with symbolic irony, since both have cast their fate with the damned. The forest through which Goodman travels also has a symbolic purpose. The farther he walks into the forest, the more closely he identifies with his evil nature. Other symbols are far less obvious. For example, some critics have suggested that Faith's pink ribbons – being neither pure white nor a devilish red – represent her psychological state somewhere between total innocence and total depravity.

Just as Goodman Brown and Faith are symbolic characters, Miss Emily, in Faulkner's "A Rose For Emily," is a symbol and represents a disappearing way of life; the character Homer Barron represents the new century and its new ways.

Sometimes an action can be symbolic. Certainly, Ahab's fatal harpoon toss at Moby Dick is itself symbolic. In another Melville story, this time the short story, "Bartleby the Scrivener: A Story of Wall Street," the act of defiance by the main character, Bartleby, who refuses to do his work, is a symbolic renunciation of the social order.

Symbols can often be identified by the importance the author gives them. She might mention them frequently or give them a special prominence by the way they are described or treated by the characters.

Allegory

In an allegory, the story has two levels of meaning. One is literal and the other is symbolic. For example, in the medieval play, "Everyman," its characters are named Kindred and Good Deeds They represent virtues and vices. Like most allegories, the play is very clear in its intent – it is meant to teach us a lesson. Many would also classify Moby Dick as an allegory about the futility of mankind trying to impose its order and will upon a metaphysically chaotic universe.

A **fable** is very similar to an allegory; however, the characters are animals that have human traits. Like an allegory, a fable has a clear moral. The best-known fables are by Aesop.

 # Alliteration

Alliteration is a stylistic method of creating a sense of rhythm and of attracting attention to specific passages in poetry and in prose. With alliteration, the initial sounds of close words are the same. The following lines from Dylan Thomas's "Fern Hill" illustrate alliteration: "I should hear him fly with the high fields / And wake to the farm forever fled from the childless land."

Assonance and consonance are similar methods. Assonance refers to the repetition of vowel sounds while consonance refers to the repetition of consonant sounds. Both differ from alliteration because the repeated sounds do not have to be at the beginning of the words.

 # Allusion

Allusions are references to events, people, places, or ideas that are commonly known. Allusions can come from history, literature, movies, music, or any other shared part of culture. The only pre-requisite for an allusion is that it be recognizable by the majority of educated readers. Unfamiliar allusions fail to make their point because readers don't recognize them.

 # Antithesis

Another common stylistic device is the antithesis. Antithesis combines two ideas that seem contradictory in order to make a larger point. Franklin D. Roosevelt's first inaugural address in 1933 contained one of the most well-known examples of antithesis: "The only thing we have to fear is fear itself."

Hyperbole

Hyperbole is a figure of speech. It's an exaggeration used to emphasize a point. The two following lines from Ralph Waldo Emerson's "The Concord Hymn" illustrate hyperbole: "Here once the embattled farmers stood / And fired the shot heard round the world."

Theme

The theme of a work of fiction is often called its central idea. What do we mean by **central idea**? A theme in a story is a lot like the main melody in a song. Although the song might take some detours along the way and there are other parts to the song, it keeps going back to the main melody. It can be a phrase or a series of phrases. The song keeps going back to the melody and it repeats itself. In part due to repetition, the melody is memorable. Chances are, after we have heard the song, it is the melody that we remember most.

Now, let us turn our attention back to stories and themes. When an author sits down to write a story, he has a melody – a theme – in his/her head that becomes an important part of the story. As in a song, the theme finds its way throughout the story – the author seems to keep coming back to it, through the characters, symbols, narration, etc. It is the story's central idea, so it is not just revealed once and then disappears.

So what is this central idea? We know it works like the main melody and keeps turning up in the story, but what do we mean by idea? Sometimes that idea is really an issue. One of the themes in "The Adventures of Huckleberry Finn" concerns the evil of slavery. Mark Twain makes it clear that Jim, the slave, is a good person and a great friend to Huck. The idea can be a concept. For example, in "The Great Gatsby," the central idea concerns the illusion of happiness and the "American dream." Repeatedly, F. Scott Fitzgerald creates symbols, events, and characters that support this theme. Eventually, the narrator, Nick abandons his plans and returns home disillusioned by the quest for wealth and social status.

How do we determine a story's theme or central idea? Sometimes it is very clear even upon a casual reading of the story. In "Bartleby the Scrivener," for example, we can see that Bartleby has been dehumanized by his tedious and purposeless work. In the end, he dies, and Melville is warning us, the readers, of the consequence of this kind of labor.

What if the theme is less clear? We will look at traditional approaches in a moment, but try starting by asking yourself: why did the author decide to write this story? What is it that he wanted us to know or learn from it? If you ask yourself these questions while you are reading – or look back at a story you have just finished – answering those questions about the motivation of the author can help reveal the theme or central idea – the "why" about this story.

A long or complex story can sometimes have more than one theme. The theme goes beyond the plot or the subject of the story to raise an issue or general idea that applies to people in the real world. To find a theme, try to generalize the particular characters and events of a story to find the values, ideas or human situations they suggest.

After you have thought about the author's purpose in writing the story and you have looked at plot, character, setting, point of view, tone, style, and symbolism, what can you do if you are still not sure of the theme? Here are a few more methods you can try:

- The title itself can often provide direction. For example, "Bartleby the Scrivener: A Story of Wall Street" gives us a good indication about the theme.
- Look for commentaries in the story by the narrator. The narrator will frequently discuss thematic issues or ideas.
- In keeping with our comparison of story theme and melody, look for patterns of repetition. Words, phrases, or events that repeat themselves often are important to the theme.
- Generalize the characters and events and ask if there is symbolism that supports your interpretation of theme.
- As we noted with regard to symbolism, sometimes a thing is just a thing – it can be dangerous to try to force a special meaning on something when it is not there. When your ideas about a theme begin to emerge, check back to the story to pick out those elements that support your conclusions. Good literary critics are like perceptive detectives. They find the right evidence to support their ideas. Also, keep in mind that a story can be interpreted in more than one way. Differences in readers' backgrounds and culture can result in different interpretations of the same story. That is one of the fascinating aspects of literature – our ideas about it are always open to discussion.

Reading the Novel

Many of the literary terms and insight that we have discussed this far apply to the novel as well as to short stories. The main difference is that a novel is considerably longer than a short story – sometimes very much longer. Another literary form, the novella, fits somewhere in length between a long short story and most novels. Like a short story, a novel has plot, character, setting, tone, point of view, style, symbols, and theme. Your analysis of those elements would be very similar to what you would do after reading a short story.

So how is a novel different from a short story, besides just being longer? In part due its length, novels often can have a more complex plot and explore more than one theme. In "The Scarlet Letter," for example, Hawthorne explores the themes of social morality, guilt, and redemption. A novel also sometimes introduces a greater number of characters, many of which can be fully developed or round characters.

Because of its length, it is often hard to know what to look for, other than its plot. Here are a few tips:

- **Carefully read the first chapter in the novel.** Many authors introduce most of their themes at the beginning of the novel. Ask yourself: Why is the author starting with this event? What is the significance of introducing these characters now instead of later? What point of view and tone is the author trying to establish? Are there any clues as to the themes that will be developed?

- **Look for repetition.** Any patterns in detail, words, and events are important.

- **Look for symbolism.** What words, phrases or images repeat themselves? Are characters or objects treated in a special way through the author's exposition or narration?

- **Read the last chapter carefully.** We often get very important clues about the themes in the story by how the author ends the novel. In the process of putting the finishing touches on the story, the author will also clarify any ambiguity or uncertainty about the theme.

Plot Summary of Moby Dick

Long considered one of the great American novels, "Moby Dick" is an epic tale about an obsessive whaling captain and his relentless quest to vanquish a dangerous white whale named Moby Dick. Published by Herman Melville in 1851, the story begins as our narrator, Ishmael, arrives in New Bedford, Massachusetts, on his way towards the whaling port on Nantucket. While in New Bedford he meets a Queequeg, a dangerous-looking harpooner from New Zealand who eventually becomes Ishmael's friend and shipmate on the Pequod. The following day at a church service Ishmael hears Father Mapple deliver a sermon about Jonah and the whale. The story, says the preacher, is a lesson about telling the truth in the face of falsehood.

On Nantucket, Ishmael and Queequeg choose among three whaling ships and decide to sign on to the Pequod. The ship is owned by two Quakers: Peleg, who is also the former captain, and Bildad. Peleg describes the new ship's captain, Ahab, as a man both ungodly and grand. We are also introduced to other important characters: Starbuck, the first mate; Stubb, the second mate; Flask the third mate; and to two harpooners, Tashtego and Daggoo. It is not until the Pequod is underway that we meet the main character, Ahab, an imposing man with a fake leg made of whalebone. We find out later that it is the killer whale, Moby Dick, which took Ahab's leg in a fierce encounter years before. Starbuck tells Ahab that his obsession with Moby Dick is madness. Ahab answers that all things are masks for something else and that man must strike through the mask to find the truth behind it. Moby Dick represents that mask to Ahab. Starbuck worries that his mad captain will lead the Pequod to a tragic ending.

As it sails around the world, the Pequod encounters numerous dangerous whales, fierce storms, and other whaling ships. In one encounter, Ahab asks the crew if it has seen Moby Dick, but he does not hear their answer. In another meeting, the ship's captain warns Ahab about Moby Dick. A crew member on a British ship named Dr. Bunger warns Ahab to leave Moby Dick alone. Despite these warnings, Ahab continues after the whale. After meeting the French ship, Rosebud, one of the Pequod's crew, a young black man named Pip, becomes frightened while lowering a boat, jumps, and gets tangled in the whale line. He is reprimanded by second mate, Stubb, and told that if it happens again he will be left at sea. When it does happen a second time, Pip is cut from the line and only survives because he is rescued by another boat. He is so traumatized by the event that he goes crazy.

Ahab also seems to be losing his mind. After his leg breaks and a carpenter tries to fix it, he angrily berates the carpenter. Later, after Starbuck reports to Ahab that the casks have sprung a leak, Ahab becomes so incensed that he pulls a musket on Starbuck. After entering the Pacific Ocean, Ahab commands the blacksmith to make him a special harpoon for use against Moby Dick. According to Ahab, the weapon is "baptized" in the name of the devil with the blood of the ship's pagan harpooners. As further evidence of his deteriorating mental state, Ahab dreams of hearses and proclaims his immortality.

At this point, Ahab needs to choose between an easy route back to Nantucket, or continuing his pursuit of Moby Dick. He decides to continue his quest. In the meantime, the Pequod sails into a violent typhoon and its compass is thrown out of alignment. Starbuck goes to tell Ahab about the compass but finds his captain asleep. He considers shooting him but decides against it and hears Ahab cry out, "Moby Dick, I clutch thy heart at last."

After fixing the compass, Ahab meets another ship, the Rachel, whose captain knows him. Captain Gardiner asks for help searching for his son, who might be lost at sea. Ahab turns down the request because he learns that Moby Dick is nearby. The last ship that the Pequod meets is the Delight. The ship recently encountered Moby Dick and was nearly destroyed in the battle. Before finally reaching the whale, Ahab admits that he has chased Moby Dick more as a demon than as a man.

The battle between Ahab and the great white whale lasts for three days. On the first day Ahab and others lower their boats and row after it. Moby Dick attacks and sinks Ahab's boat. He is rescued by Stubb's boat. On the second day, the same thing happens – Ahab's boat is sunk. The whale has also broken Ahab's ivory leg. With two failed attempts behind them, Starbuck assails Ahab for his "blasphemous" fixation on the whale and declares that they will all be dragged to the bottom of the sea. Ahab answers that the whole battle is "immutably decreed" and calls himself "Fate's lieutenant." When they reach the whale on the third day, Ahab stabs Moby Dick with his harpoon but the whale attacks the Pequod and it starts sinking. In desperation, Ahab tosses his harpoon again at Moby Dick but becomes tangled in the line and goes down with it. Ishmael survives the attack only because he is on a whaling boat instead of the Pequod. He is rescued by the captain of the Rachel, who has lost his son to the sea only to take in another orphan.

Plot Summary of The Scarlet Letter

A classic of American literature, "The Scarlet Letter" by Nathaniel Hawthorne is a psychological drama that explores the themes of public morality, shame, religion and redemption. The story is set in Puritan Boston where a young married woman named Hester Prynne is accused of committing adultery. In keeping with the Puritan tradition of publicly shaming sinners, she is being led to a scaffold in the town marketplace. On the front of her gown is an elaborately embroidered letter "A" that she is forced to wear at all times as a reminder of her sin. Her daughter, Pearl, is with her. On the scaffold, she is commanded to reveal the name of her adulterous partner – Pearl's father – but refuses to do so. Watching from a distance in the crowd is her husband, Roger Chillingworth, who has returned to Boston following a long captivity with an Indian tribe.

Chillingworth visits Hester after she is returned to jail and pledges to discover the name of Pearl's father. He swears that he will see the truth written on the man's heart. He also demands that Hester never reveal his identity to anyone. Following her release Hester moves with Pearl into a cottage near the edge of the woods. There she lives a quiet life and spends her time helping the poor and infirm. She earns a modest living doing stitch work for town officials. Her daughter, Pearl, becomes something of a wild child and refuses to obey her mother. Her husband, meanwhile, gains recognition as a good physician and is eventually assigned to care for Arthur Dimmesdale, an ailing minister. Chillingworth discovers that Dimmesdale is in fact Pearl's father and pledges to torment the minister for his sin.

The weight of his guilt and shame eventually compels Dimmesdale to go to the scaffold where Hester had been publicly humiliated. In his imagination, he envisions the entire town watching him and seeing a letter on his chest. Both Hester and Pearl come to the scaffold and stand with Dimmesdale. A meteor passes through the night sky and illuminates the three of them. They can see Chillingworth off in the distance watching them. Dimmesdale tells Hester that he is afraid of Chillingworth. Hester begins to understand that her husband is tormenting and gradually killing Dimmesdale. She decides to do what she can to protect him.

Weeks later, she sees Chillingworth in the woods and tells him that she will reveal his true identity to Dimmesdale. The next time she meets Dimmesdale she does tell him the truth. He is angry and hurt but Hester talks him into running away with her. She arranges passage on a ship that is departing the day after Dimmesdale is to give an important sermon. Chillingworth, meanwhile, talks the ship's captain into letting him on the boat as well. Dimmesdale's sermon is a tremendous success and considered the best he has ever given. Afterwards he walks over to the scaffold and – standing before the crowd – asks Hester and Pearl to join him. Chillingworth tries to stop this but Hester and Pearl go up to the scaffold. With the two of them beside him, Dimmesdale tells the crowd that he is a sinner just like Hester and that he should have stood beside her years before when she was publicly humiliated. Dimmesdale tears open his shirt and reveals the scarlet letter "A" on his flesh. He then falls to his knees and dies.

Hester and Pearl leave Boston and then Hester returns several years later, but without Pearl. People believe that she has gotten married and is living in Europe. Hester, meanwhile, keeps wearing her scarlet letter. When she dies, she is buried in King's Chapel.

 # Plot Summary of The Great Gatsby

Written by F. Scott Fitzgerald, "The Great Gatsby" is a story about hope, disillusionment, and the American Dream. It is the summer of 1922. The narrator and main character is Nick Carraway, a young Yale graduate who has moved to New York from the Midwest to learn about the bond business. Nick rents a home in the wealthy but socially unfashionable town of West Egg on Long Island. Although financially successful, most residents of West Egg are newly rich and are not considered part of the established upper class. One of those residents is Nick's neighbor, Jay Gatsby, a mysterious businessman who claims he came from a wealthy Midwestern family – "now all dead" – and was educated at Oxford, England. Gatsby lives in an impressively decorated mansion, throws extravagant parties, and proudly displays the symbols of his material success.

Nick's cousin, Daisy Buchanan, lives across the bay in the town of East Egg with her husband, Tom. East Egg is where the elite and "old money" live. One evening Nick drives to East Egg for dinner with the Buchanans. They introduce him to a beautiful woman named Jordan Baker. Nick and Jordan soon become romantically involved. After receiving one of Gatsby's coveted party invitations, Nick sees Jordan at the party and together they meet Gatsby. After getting Jordan alone, Gatsby confesses that he knew Daisy when they were in Louisville and is still madly in love with her. In a poignant glimpse into his true feelings, Gatsby tells Jordon that he often sits in his mansion staring across the bay at the green light at the end of Daisy's dock. At Gatsby's request,

Nick arranges a meeting at his house between Gatsby and Daisy. Although the reunion begins awkwardly, the two eventually fall in love again and begin an affair.

Even though he is having an affair of his own with a woman named Myrtle Wilson, Tom Buchanan is incensed that Daisy is cheating on him. He insists that all of them – Gatsby, Daisy, Jordan, and Nick – drive to a hotel in New York City. There he confronts Gatsby about the affair and accuses him of bootlegging grain alcohol and participating in other illegal activities. More pointedly, Tom insists that Daisy never loved Gatsby and belittles Gatsby's pretensions to wealth and social status. Caught in the middle of the confrontation, Daisy becomes confused about her real feelings towards Gatsby and her husband. Eventually, she realizes that her fate is to be with Tom. In a gesture of contempt towards Gatsby, Tom has Gatsby drive Daisy home to East Egg, as if to prove that he no longer fears Gatsby's influence over his wife.

In a separate car, Nick, Jordan, and Tom drive back to Long Island. Along the way, they come across an accident. While driving through the "valley of the ashes" – a lower class industrial area between Long Island and New York City – Gatsby's car has struck and killed Tom's lover, Myrtle Wilson. Even though Daisy was driving, Gatsby tells Nick that he will take the blame. The following day, Myrtle's husband, George, decides that whoever killed his wife was also her lover. He believes that she ran out to the road to stop her lover's car, the car hit her and drove on. Consumed with grief, George goes out to West Egg and asks for directions to Gatsby's house. He finds Gatsby at the pool, shoots and kills him, and then turns the gun on himself.

As the story ends, Nick discovers that it was Tom who told George Wilson where to find Gatsby. Nick is disgusted and disillusioned by his experiences in New York and decides to return to the Midwest. He ends his relationship with Jordan Baker. In a final tribute to Gatsby and the dream for which he lived and died, Nick stands on Gatsby's beach looking across the bay at the green light at the end of Daisy's dock.

Plot Summary of The Last of the Mohicans

Written by James Fenimore Cooper, one of America's first important novelists, "The Last of the Mohicans" is a historical romance that takes place during the French and Indian Wars. The English and French had long been adversaries in Europe; their age-old conflict inevitably followed the French and English colonists to the New World. Taking advantage of local tribal rivalries, the French persuaded the Iroquois and Huron tribes to become allies and help defeat the English. As the story begins, Major Duncan Heyward is escorting two sisters, Cora and Alice Munro, through the dangerous forests to Fort William Henry where their father is stationed. Their guide is a Huron named Magua. On the way to Fort Henry, the group is joined by David Gainut, a psalm singer. Behind them, a young Mohican named Uncas is watching and tracking their footsteps.

Uncas and his father, Chingachgook, are the only survivors of what was once the great Mohican tribe. They have befriended a seasoned English scout and frontiersman named Natty Bumppo, known by most as Hawkeye. After discovering the Huron by hiding in the woods, Uncas returns to tell his father and Hawkeye. They decide that Magua is deliberately leading Duncan and the women in the wrong direction. They confront Magua and a fight ensues. Although Hawkeye manages to shoot Magua in the shoulder, the wounded Huron chief escapes into the woods before they capture him.

Fearing the inevitable return of Magua and his warriors, the group spends the night in an island cave. A bloody skirmish takes place the next morning; Hawkeye and the Mohicans escape but David, Duncan, Cora and Alice are all captured by Magua. The Huron chief tells Cora that he will let the others go if she marries him. When she refuses, he decides that all the captives should die. As Duncan tries to kill one of the Huron warriors, a shot rings out: it is Hawkeye and his two Mohican friends. They battle Magua and his warriors and kill two of them. Magua pretends to be dead and manages to sneak away.

After several more close calls with the Hurons, Hawkeye and his fellow travelers eventually manage to get to Fort William Henry. Colonel Munro comes out and welcomes his daughters. The English ask for a truce. Munro is told there will be no reinforcements from Fort Edward. Munro accepts the terms of surrender and the women and children start to evacuate Fort Henry. Suddenly, with Magua urging them on, the French Indian allies brutally massacre the retreating soldiers, as well as the innocent women and children. David Gamut saves the lives of the two Munro sisters from the slaughter but both women are taken by Magua. Gamut follows them.

Hawkeye and his companions track down the two women. Magua has brought Alice to a Huron village and left Alice at a Delaware village. Using a variety of clever disguises, Hawkeye and his companions manage to recapture Alice, at which point Duncan professes his romantic feelings for her. When Magua discovers that Alice is missing, he goes to the second village to take possession of his wife-to-be, Cora. Uncas, who had been captured by the Hurons and then freed by Hawkeye, gets to the Delaware village before Magua but is unable to convince the tribe's leader to free Cora. Magua then escapes with her into the forest. A chase and a battle then follow. The Hurons are defeated, but Magua escapes up a mountain with Cora and a few braves. Hawkeye, Uncas, and Duncan follow quickly behind Magua. Uncas, who has managed to climb above Cora and Magua, jumps down to save her but as he leaps she is slain by another Huron. Magua is angered by her death and moves to kill the Huron. Uncas, tragically, has landed between them and Magua kills the last of the Mohicans.

Magua tries to escape by climbing farther up the mountain. He leaps across several fissures but finally lands short and barely manages to hold on to a small tree. From below, Hawkeye aims his rifle at Magua, a shot rings out, and the enemy Huron falls headlong to his death. Uncas and Cora are buried next to each other in the woods. Chingachgook mourns the death of his son, Uncas, as the Delaware sage Tamenund proclaims, "I have lived to see the last warrior of the wise race of the Mohicans."

Plot Summary of The Adventures of Huckleberry Finn

One of America's best-loved fictional characters, Huck Finn is both the narrator and central character of "The Adventures of Huckleberry Finn," Mark Twain's sequel to "The Adventures of Tom Sawyer." Both novels are set in St. Petersburg, Missouri, along the banks of the Mississippi River. Both novels use humor, satire, and a page-turning plot to keep readers engaged, while at the same time upending many Southern traditions. In the earlier novel, Huck and Tom had discovered $12,000 in treasure, which is invested for them by Judge Thatcher. This new series of adventures begins when Huck decides to run away from home. Adopted by the Widow Douglas and Miss Watson, Huck feels dissatisfied with his new "civilized" life. He meets up with his long-time friend, Tom Sawyer, who promises to start a new band of robbers. Although they have the perfect hideout in a cave near the river, most of the young robbers get bored with their make-believe battles and the group falls apart. When Huck sees some footprints in the snow, he is sure they belong to his Pa, who has come back to get his share of the money that Huck and Tom discovered.

Eventually, Pa catches up with Huck, takes a dollar from him as his payment, and then locks Huck in a cabin to keep him from going back to the Widow. At first Huck likes this new arrangement but soon gets tired of his Pa's beatings. He comes up with a clever plan of action: he decides to stage his own murder by killing a pig and then spreading the blood around as if it were his own. He then takes a canoe down river until he gets to Jackson Island. While he is there, he spots a camp that belongs to Miss Watson's runaway slave, Jim. At first, Jim is frightened by Huck because he is supposed to be dead, but then decides he likes having Huck as his companion.

When the river starts to rise and a whole house floats by the island, Jim and Huck decide to take a look and go aboard. In a corner of the house lies a dead man; Jim believes it is Pa but refuses to tell Huck. After disguising himself as a girl and going into town, Huck learns that Jim and his Pa are suspected of murdering him and that they believe Jim is hiding on Jackson Island. Huck hurries back to Jim and they take a large raft down river at night and hide during the day. Along the way, they come upon a steamboat that has crashed. They go aboard and discover three thieves, two of which are discussing killing the third. Huck and Jim try to escape but find their raft gone, so they steal a skiff that belonged to the thieves. They do escape but the steamboat floats down the river, so low in the water it is clear that everyone on board has drowned. As their journey down the Mississippi River continues, Huck and Jim become close friends

Huck and Jim decide they need to get to Cairo so they can take a boat up the Ohio River and into the free states. When they become separated during a dense fog, Jim drifts along on the raft and Huck in the canoe. They end up going past Cairo. On the raft again, they are run over by a steamboat and are forced to jump overboard. After swimming to shore, Huck is eventually invited to go live with the Grangerford family. Jim hides in a swamp. Huck is happy for a while but discovers there is a feud between this new family and another one called the Sheperdsons. Following a battle between the two families, all the males are killed, so Huck runs back to the river and finds Jim. The two take off down river once again and rescue two scam artists known as the Duke and the King. They eventually take over the raft from Huck and Jim.

The Duke and the King learn that three orphaned girls stand to inherit a large sum of money and pretend to be their British uncles. Huck likes the girls and wants no part of this scheme. He sneaks into the King's room and steals the gold from the inheritance and hides it in the coffin of Peter Wilks, the con men's deceased brother. When he sees one of the girls crying, he tells her the truth about the scam. She decides to leave the house for a few days so that Huck can escape. Soon after she leaves, the real uncles arrive but they have lost their luggage and cannot prove who they are. As the dispute about everyone's real identity continues, one of the real uncles says that the dead brother, Peter Wilks, had a tattoo on his chest and challenges the King to identify it. To decide who is telling the truth, they dig up Peter Wilks' grave and find the gold that Huck had stashed inside. In the ruckus that follows, Huck goes back to Jim and the raft. They start down the river but the Duke and King catch up with them and take over the raft again. Claiming he is a runaway slave, they sell Jim into slavery.

Huck is anxious to free Jim and goes to the home of the person who is keeping him. By coincidence, it happens to be Tom Sawyer's Aunt Sally and so Huck pretends to be Tom. Then the real Tom arrives and he pretends to be his own younger brother, Sid. Working as a team again, Tom and Huck figure out a way to free Jim by telling the town that a group of thieves planned to steal him. One night they manage to get Jim and start running off, a group of local farmers following and shooting after them. Tom is hit in the leg by a bullet and Huck goes off to get a doctor. The doctor finds where Tom is hiding with Jim and comes back with Jim in irons and Tom on a stretcher. When Tom awakes, he demands that Jim be set free again.

In the meantime, Aunt Polly shows up and says that Jim is really a free man because the Widow passed away and freed him in her will. Huck and Tom are delighted and give

Jim $40 for being such a great prisoner and letting them free him. Jim tells Huck that it was his Pa who was the dead man in the floating house. Aunt Sally then offers to take in Huck, but he refuses on the grounds that he already tried that way of life. The story ends with Huck admitting that he would never have started his book if he had known it would take so long to write it.

Understanding Poetry

Someone once said that poetry is to prose what dancing is to walking. It is an apt analogy. Poetry, like prose, uses words. However, whereas we find most prose fairly easy to read and comprehend, poetry uses words in quite a different way. That difference makes poetry both a special art form and a challenge for most of us to read.

So what is it about poetry that makes it different from prose (like the prose you are reading now)? Keep in mind that there are as many forms or approaches to writing poems as there are poets, so however we define poetry is bound to be a generalization. For starters, we can say that most poems use a form of compression of thought and imagery. Think of the process that it takes to create a diamond – the compression of raw earth into coal and then into a diamond. The poet typically compresses "the message" into powerful images and phrases. So, while prose permits us to catch up with its message as we casually walk along with it, poetry is compact. That is part of its power and beauty.

Because poetry is a compression of thought and image, the way words are used is different from prose, too. Every word counts. Poets are typically very sensitive to the meanings – and double meanings – of words, as well as the way they sound, the way they look on the page, and the way they sound when spoken aloud. That leads us to another way to describe poetry.

Poetry is closely related to music in the way that it uses expressive language, sounds, and rhythms. As the English poet Samuel Taylor Coleridge put it, "The man that hath not music in his soul can indeed never be a genuine poet." Most poetry is meant to be heard, as is music. Whenever you can, read a poem aloud. Much of its meaning can be found in the way that the words sound as well as rhymes that may not be as apparent when reading silently.

Again, we should emphasize that no two poems are alike – some poems read like long lines of prose and some are not at all musical. On the page the poem looks like it is walking, not dancing. Nevertheless, rules are made to be broken, and many poets, being playful types, love to break the rules. It also bears mentioning that a poem written two hundred years ago – while as artful and potentially enjoyable as any written today – can be a special challenge due to the changes in our language and literary techniques.

So where should you start if you are trying to "get" a poem?

Start by not trying. By that we mean, don't start by trying to figure out the poem. Just read it, preferably aloud, and see what images or ideas break through. What phrases or words strike you as particularly powerful or funny or just thought provoking?

Go back a second time and take note of any words or phrases that you do not understand. In older poems especially the poet might use words, contractions, or phrases that are not in common use anymore. Find out what they mean. Poetry often needs to be interpreted line by line, slowly and patiently.

Ask yourself: what is this poem about? Is it about love? Nature? A philosophical perspective? A personal experience that had a profound and lasting impact on the poet's life? What does the poet want you to think or feel after reading the poem? Why did the poet write this poem?

If the meaning of a poem is not immediately clear to you, try not to feel frustrated. As T.S. Eliot once said, "Genuine poetry can communicate before it is understood." What he means is that the language itself – the music, the placement of the words, the images – already tells you something even before you have the poem "figured out."

Another way to better understand a poem is to know something about the poet and the historical period when the poem was written. As with stories, the social, historical, and cultural context of a poem often play an important role in its creation and understanding.

Try to keep an open mind about the poems you read. The less you impose your own expectations about what poetry is supposed to be like, the more you are likely to understand and enjoy what you are reading.

Read the following poems:

"Barbara Allen" at: http://www.sacred-texts.com/neu/eng/child/ch084.htm

"Crazy Jane Talks with the Bishop" at http://www.web-books.com/Classics/Poetry/Anthology/Yeats/Crazy.htm

"Ode on a Grecian Urn" http://www.bartleby.com/101/625.html

"The Road Not Taken" at http://www.bartleby.com/119/1.html

"The Love Song of J. Alfred Prufrock" at http://www.bartleby.com/198/1.html

Read some of Shakespeare's poetry. Visit Bartleby Online for an extensive choice of Shakespeare's poems and plays. http://www.bartleby.com/people/Shakespe.html

Analyzing Poetry

A **haiku** is a poem that is 17 syllables long, unrhymed, with three lines total in this order: five syllables, seven syllables, five syllables. Here is an example:

> Wander deeply now
> Find knowledge, be determined
> Pass test, save money.

A **rhyme** is two lines that end in similarly sounding words. When the words look alike but don't rhyme it is called an **eye rhyme**.

A group of lines in a poem is called a **stanza**.

Each letter represents a line in the poem that rhymes. Here is an example. Read the following poem and assign a letter to each rhyming end word. A new rhyme should take on a new letter.

> Awhile ago a good friend asked me,
> "Will you ever get serious and who will he be?"
> I shrugged my shoulders and moved along,
> But it wasn't that long…
> There's been something up for quite awhile,
> Makes me laugh and makes me smile.
> I know this feeling-I know how it seems,
> I've felt this but only in my dreams.
> I never thought I'd be serious for anyone,
> But still-I didn't know that's how it'd become.
> I wasn't looking for a long lost love,
> I wasn't looking for someone to think of.
> Happiness has come my way,
> Now I don't know what to say.
> I didn't realized what was wrong,
> I'd been missing something all along.

Now compare your answers with mine:

> Awhile ago a good friend asked me, **A**
> "Will you ever get serious and who will he be?" **A**
> I shrugged my shoulders and moved along, **B**
> But it wasn't that long…**B**

There's been something up for quite awhile, **C**
Makes me laugh and makes me smile. **C**
I know this feeling-I know how it seems, **D**
I've felt this but only in my dreams. **D**
I never thought I'd be serious for anyone, **E**
But still-I didn't know that's how it'd become. **E**
I wasn't looking for a long lost love, **F**
I wasn't looking for someone to think of. **F**
Happiness has come my way, **G**
Now I don't know what to say. **G**
I didn't realized what was wrong, **B**
I'd been missing something all along. **B**

Now, a couplet pattern would look like this: AABBCCDDEE. Every two lines would rhyme. If there are three lines in a stanza it's called a triplet. Four lines in a stanza and it is a quatrain.

There are different types of meter. A line in a poem is named for the number of feet it contains: monometer: one foot, dimeter: two feet, trimeter: three feet, tetrameter: four feet, pentameter: five feet, hexameter: six feet, heptameter: seven feet. Iambic Pentameter is the most common.

When a poem doesn't rhyme it is called **blank verse.**

Free verse is a poem in whatever format you want.

A **sonnet** is a rhymed, metered poem which is 14 lines long.

Epic is a long, narrative poem that tells a story. A good example is ***Beowulf***, an epic, early English poem in which Beowulf kills Grendel (a monster). He then kills another monster and dies.

Limerick is a nonsense poem, with five lines. Lines 1 and 2 rhyme, 3 and 4 rhyme and line 5 rhymes with line 1.

An **elegy** is to memorialize someone.

An **epigram** are used to create a brief, humorous or memorable statement in poetry. They are used to convey satire or can be purposefully confusing. Their purpose is to get the reader's attention through humor or more careful examination. Not all epigrams appear in poetry although Shakespeare, and Blake in particular were famous for using them.

Examples include:

"Little strokes/Fell great oaks." - Benjamin Franklin

"Here's my wife: here let her lie! Now she's at rest-and so am I." - John Dryden

Some famous non-poetry epigrams include:

"If you can't be a good example, you'll just have to be a horrible warning." - Catherine the Great

"It is better to light a candle than curse the darkness." - Eleanor Roosevelt

Voice

Voice is another word for narrator. Voice differs slightly from narration because there is a person or personality talking or telling the story. Voice is heavily linked with tone. Is the tone/voice cheerful, depressing, outraged, etc?

A good illustration of these ideas is Emily Dickinson's poem, "I'm Nobody! Who Are You?" at: http://www.bartleby.com/113/1027.html. Is the speaker in this poem a man or a woman? Can you tell anything about the speaker's circumstances or mood?

Word Choice and Word Order

"Word choice" refers to the words used in the poem. It sounds simple and perhaps obvious, but because poetry relies so much on compression, word choice is extremely important. Every word in a poem counts. Indeed, some so-called minimalist poets like Robert Creeley might have one or two words on a line, each one powerfully placed to give it extra emphasis. Words are chosen not only for what they mean, but how they sound, how they look on the page, how they advance the poem into the next word or phrase. There are also poetic structures – rhythms and rhymes – that make one word a better choice than another. Even in modern poems, which at first glance appear unstructured and the language random, there are internal rhythms that guide the poet's choice of words.

Consider these two lines from T.S. Eliot's "The Love Song of J. Alfred Prufrock":

I should have been a pair of ragged claws
Scuttling across the floors of silent seas.

In addition to the striking imagery, notice how Eliot's choice of words retains a five beat emphasis in both lines, while creating an alliterative s-sound in the last line with the words "scuttling, floors, silent, and seas."

"Word order" is exactly what it sounds like, the order words are arranged in the poem. Most modern poems use a conventional sentence structure of subject – verb – object. However, to achieve certain poetic effects or emphasis, modern poets often will upend traditional word order or use the length of the poetic line to give words greater impact.

The idiosyncratic American poet, E.E. Cummings, starts a poem with the line: "All in green went my love riding." (As with many of Cummings' poems, the first line is also the title of the poem.) If he had used conventional word order, he might have written the line: "My love went riding all in green." Changing the word order makes these rather ordinary words more powerful. It also opens the line to a variety of new interpretations. Was his love riding while dressed in green clothing? Or was his love riding through a forest or woods all in green?

Imagery

People say a picture is worth a thousand words. That is certainly true in poetry. Poets are word painters – they use language to create pictures or images to help express the idea of the poem. The term "imagery" refers to language that evokes a physical sensation produced by one of the five senses: sight, hearing, taste, touch, smell. Imagery is an important tool for a poet, because it helps him establish a mood, and it may also help indicate theme.

To return to Eliot's poem, "The Love Song of J. Alfred Prufrock," consider this line: "When the evening is spread out against the sky/Like a patient etherized upon a table." In addition to the utter novelty of the image, we immediately grasp Eliot's sense of the evening sky and can visualize a real patient lying on a table.

At the start of the twentieth century, a group of poets in England, Europe, and the United States was known as "Imagists." Their goal was to write poetry that did not send a particular message or idea. They believed that because objective truth did not exist, everything had to be perceived anew – as if seen for the first time. Their poems presented strong images that were meant to stand on their own. One example comes from a proponent of Imagism named Ezra Pound and is called "In a Station of the Metro," at: http://www.internal.org/list_poems.phtml?authorID=1 .

The poem is only two lines long and compares two contrasting images. What is he contrasting?

The American poet, William Carlos Williams, was also influenced by the Imagists. Although he used their technique of presenting sparse but powerful images, Williams also believed that powerful images should be used to communicate ideas. "The Red Wheelbarrow," at: http://www.english.upenn.edu/~afilreis/88/wcw-red-wheel.html, is a good example of his approach. His work has been called "anti-poetic." In reading this poem, one can understand why: we have two simple images, one of the red wheelbarrow, the other of the white chickens. Both are prefaced by the lines that "so much depends/ upon…" a clear indication that these artifacts of farm life are more than just objects.

A medical general practitioner who wrote poetry in his spare time, Williams was influenced by the artistic and literary movements of his day. In particular, he was influenced by a group of painters led by Pablo Picasso called the Cubists. The Cubists believed that all truth is subjective, a philosophical position that sprang from a disenchantment with the traditional beliefs of Western culture. Until then, painting had been a way to capture and express the Truth. All we have to rely on is what we see. So Truth is subjective – actually, the accumulation of subjective truths.

If you study some of Picasso's paintings, you will see images of people who appear deformed: they have multiple pairs of eyes, noses that seem to be in the wrong place. This is Picasso's way of telling us that there is no such thing as absolute truth. Truth is based on our perspective. Williams is suggesting the same idea. "The Red Wheelbarrow" presents us with two objects: a wheelbarrow and some chickens. "So much depends upon" that wheelbarrow because the truth is wherever and however we want to see it. This is another great example of showing the importance of knowing the circumstances of a writer and the time period of their work.

Figures of Speech

One way that poets achieve the level of powerful compression found in many poems is by using **figures of speech**. It is a way of describing one thing in terms of something else. Common figures of speech include metaphors, similes, and personification. Poets use them to express an idea or image.

A **simile** is a comparison between two different items that includes the words "like" or "as." Our earlier reference to the T.S. Eliot line about the evening sky being "like a patient etherized upon a table" is an example of a simile.

A **metaphor** is a comparison between two things without using the words "like" or "as." In another Williams poem, "Portrait of a Lady," he writes: "Your thighs are appletrees." He does not say they are like appletrees but that they are appletrees. That is a metaphor.

Personification is giving human characteristics to inanimate objects.

Epithet is an adjective or phrase that used to express a characteristic of a thing or a person such as Alexander the Great. Homer and Keats used epithets so regularly that they became part of common language such as "gray-eyed Athena." In current context, epithets are generally thought of as having a negative connotation such as the term "racial epithets."

Symbolism

A "symbol" is a thing, person, or event that represents an idea. A red traffic light is a symbol that means to stop (or speed up if you like taking chances). In poetry, symbols are not usually as overt as that. They are subject to multiple interpretations.

The Irish poet, William Butler Yeats, uses the symbolic image of the falcon in "The Second Coming," He writes, "The falcon cannot hear the falconer." Of course, the symbolism depends upon our knowing something about the relationship between the falcon and the falconer. The falconer is a person who trains falcons to fly, catch prey and return. Without that knowledge, the symbolism is hard to grasp. We are helped by other images and symbols – and outright statements – in the poem. Yeats was writing at a time of great pessimism about the state of the world. His poem uses several images and symbols of decay and destruction. In another line he says, "Mere anarchy is loosed upon the world."

Of course, if you are of the "glass half full" school, the falcon might also be a symbol of freedom. You could make the case that all the old institutions have failed and now we are free of the falconer and can do as we please.

For other examples read "A Supermarket in California" at:
http://www.english.upenn.edu/~afilreis/88/supermarket.html and "A Dream Deferred" by Langston Hughes at: http://www.cswnet.com/~menamc/langston.htm

Reading Drama

As a literary art form, drama is unique: it is meant to be performed and seen by an audience on a stage. Reading drama requires a good imagination and the ability to visualize what is on the page, taking place on the stage.

If you have seen a play, you know that a great deal more than dialogue takes place. The lighting, scenery, the stage props – all these and more add to the experience of a play and to its meaning. So when you read, for example, Eugene O'Neill's "The Great God Brown" (http://www.gutenberg.net.au/ebooks04/0400091h.html), it is important to imagine what is happening on the stage. Who are the characters and what do they look like? What expressions do they use when they speak? How do they move on the stage? Slowly? Quickly? If there is music, how does it add to the play? Is it used to highlight certain events or characters, or is it a central element in the play itself, as in a musical? What is the stage setting? Does the lighting tell us what we should be paying attention to? Is it used to establish a mood?

In many plays, symbolism has as important a role to play as many of the characters. In Eugene O'Neill's play, "Long Day's Journey into Night," the sound of a fog horn symbolizes the state of confusion and feeling lost the main characters are experiencing. Just as in fiction and poetry, words, items, characters, and actions can be symbolic. Because drama is meant to be seen on a stage, symbolism in plays must be visual: actions, objects, or sounds that the audience can observe.

One of America's greatest playwrights, the winner of the Noble Prize for Literature as well as several Pulitzer Prizes, Eugene O'Neill was famous for pushing the visual and dramatic limits of the stage. His use of masks in "The Great God Brown" is both an homage to the early Greek playwrights and a symbolic expression of O'Neill's ideas about personality and self. Dion Anthony wears his society mask, Margaret loves him, and so does his chum Billy Brown. But the unmasked Dion is a different character – rebellious, searching, melancholy, lost. When he is without his mask, Margaret is terrified by him.

Just as a theme or central idea serves as the foundation of most fiction and poetry, playwrights also use their plays as a way to comment on issues and ideas. Ask yourself: why has the playwright written this play? What is it that the author wants us to know or learn after seeing or reading it? Try to analyze the characters symbolically as well as individually. That is, try to figure out what the characters represent, as well as what motivates them as individuals.

Writing About Drama

Writing an essay about plays is not unlike writing about novels, short stories or poems. After you create a thesis about the play, you need to support your ideas with scenes or lines from the play itself. There are a few conventions about writing about plays that you should be aware of:

First, when referring to a play, either *italicize* or underline the title: *The Great God Brown* or The Great God Brown.

When quoting a single line from a play and you mention the name of the character who is speaking in the text that introduces that line, type it all as part of the same sentence. For example, In *The Great God Brown*, Billy Brown says, "You lie! I'll have her thrown back on the street!" (12). A page number should be cited after each quote, as well.

If you are quoting an exchange of dialogue between two or more characters, you should indent, as you would for a long quote, and use no quotation marks. For example:

> MARGARET: (*proudly*) I'm glad to have three such strong boys to protect me.
> ELDEST: (*boasting*) We'd kill anyone that touched you, wouldn't we? (18)

Always cite a page number if you are quoting directly from a play and indicate which specific text you are quoting from in a Work Cited page at the end of your essay.

Plot

As with novels and short stories, plays tell their story through a series of events called a plot. The play is not just the summation of its events, anymore than a novel is just a plot. The play is about something, but the plot provides the structure for telling us what that something is.

Unlike many novels or stories that rely on a narrator to tell us what is happening, we have to see the plot unfolding on the stage. We have to rely on the characters' words and actions to know what is taking place. The author of a play does have other tools that convey plot. For example, the stage scenery and lighting can be as important as a lengthy description of a setting in a novel or short story. The actors' costumes and other props can help explain the plot and move the story back in time or into the future.

The plot of a play usually follows a conventional structure. Plays usually begin with some type of exposition where we meet the characters and are given a sense of the setting. That is usually followed with rising action, which culminates in a crisis of some kind. In the typical play, the crisis is solved by the main character. It is usually by facing and solving the crisis that the main character grows or changes in some way. Those parts of the story are called the denouement and resolution.

A subplot is a less important series of events and is developed along with the main plot. In "The Great God Brown," the use of masks allows O'Neill to develop a subplot showing the characters wearing their social masks. For O'Neill, the main plot is the disintegration of the real mask-less personalities of the characters.

The events in a play are typically divided into main "acts" and scenes within an act. An act represents a major change or advance in the plot. Scenes represent a self-contained point in time and place in which a main event occurs. "Hamlet," for example, is divided into five acts. The last act is divided into two major scenes. The first scene takes place in a churchyard where they are burying Ophelia. The second and final scene switches the location to a hall in the castle where Hamlet and Laertes have their famous duel.

 # Characters in Drama

Depending on the overall theme and purpose of a play, its characters typically appear on stage with human characteristics and traits. Of course, they are not really "real," but the play's verisimilitude and success depends on how real the characters are portrayed. In some plays, the characters are meant to be "types" or symbolic. Even in plays that allow for a great deal of psychological complexity, the characters have been created by their authors to dramatize specific ideas and themes.

In many of O'Neill's plays, the use of masks, character asides (similar to Shakespeare's soliloquies), and even characters that speak aloud their subconscious thoughts, allow a rich and complex development of character. Most plays, however, rely on the dialogue and action of the characters to give the audience necessary information. A few plays (notably, Tennessee Williams's *The Glass Menagerie*) have narrators.

As with stories, dramatic characters can be round or flat. The main characters are usually round characters whereas characters with minor roles would be considered flat characters. Some characters exist in a play as a foil, as a means of advancing our understanding of a major character.

Certainly the most accessible way to understand a character is by what the character says and does. While most speech in a play consists of dialogue – an exchange with one or more characters – you will also hear monologues and soliloquies. A monologue is speech by one character while the other characters are on stage. Another kind of speech is called a soliloquy; it is speech meant to be heard by the audience and not by the other characters on stage. In most instances, a soliloquy is given while the character is alone on stage.

On stage, the only way a character can express thought is through dialogue or action. In one of Hamlet's soliloquies we get to learn what is taking place behind the facade of madness that he is showing to the other characters. An "aside" is another way for a character to give the audience information that is being hidden from the other characters. In an aside, the character speaks directly to the audience or to himself, while turned away from the other characters. The others on stage do not hear this speech.

Just as our own use of language – how we write and speak – can tell people a lot about who we are, the character's speech in a play does so as well. Is the character speaking formally, informally? Can you tell by the way the character speaks how she feels about something – a problem, another character? Is what the character says consistent, or does he say one thing to one character or something else to another? O'Neill is famous for having his characters speak at two different levels: one for the outside world and one for the inner self. Like words, a character's actions tell us a great deal about who the character really is – his values, beliefs, and personality. Sometimes what a character does is different from what he says. In Hamlet, for example, outwardly he pretends to be crazy in order to fool the King but we know from his words that he really is not.

Staging

The look, sound and feel of a play are created by its "staging." Some of the elements of staging include:

- **Scenery:** When the curtain goes up, the first thing that an audience sees is the scenery. In "The Great God Brown," the play opens showing a pier by a casino. A rail encloses the entire wharf in the back. It is a moonlit night in the middle of June. The players can hear a quartet singing "Sweet Adeline" from the casino. It is Billy Brown's graduation from high school, and although the background is romantic and pretty, O'Neill contrasts Billy's parents' unkempt, "dumpy" appearance with the setting.

- **Props:** These are the items – "properties" – that are put on stage for the actors to use. Props can be useful – a cup of coffee – or symbolic, like the skull Hamlet lifts out of a grave.

- **Costumes:** What the characters are wearing can tell us much about the historical setting of the play, as well as the social background of the characters. For example, Billy's mother in the opening scene is described as "dumpy and overdressed," suggesting her lack of sophistication.

- **Music:** A play can use music to help create a mood or it can be used as an active element that involves the characters directly. In "The Great God Brown," Billy's mother comments that the song, "Sweet Adeline" is being poorly sung and would be improved if her son, Billy, were in the quartet.

- **Sound effects:** These are sounds other than the play's music or the characters' speech.

If you go to see a play, you will be able to see and hear all these staging effects taking place. If you are reading a play, you will find the stage directions and descriptions that the author has provided to create the type of setting she wants. In Eugene O'Neill's plays, these directions and instructions are elaborate and very specific.

The Oedipus Trilogy

The plot of "Oedipus Rex" can be thought of as a detective story. The story is about a detective secure in his own virtue and sense of duty who tries to discover who committed an awful crime only to find out it is himself. The more he learns about his crime the more terrible it appears to be to him. He has committed terrible crimes against society and terrible sins against the gods.

Oedipus was born to King Laius and Queen Jocasta of Thebes. The king and queen were warned by an oracle that Oedipus would grow up and murder his father and marry his mother, so they gave him to a servant to be left in the wilderness to die. The servant did as instructed but Oedipus was discovered by a peasant, who then gave him to his master and mistress. They raised Oedipus as their own son, not knowing who he really was. Many years passed. King Laius was on his way to Delphi and met a young man along the road. The two argued with each other and Oedipus killed Laius. He did not know that the man was his father.

Thebes was soon confronted by the Sphinx, a monster that had the body of a lion and the head of a woman. After Oedipus solved a difficult riddle posed by the Sphinx, the people of Thebes made Oedipus their king. Their queen, Jocasta, was given to him as his wife. Thus, the second prediction of the oracle came true and Oedipus unknowingly married his mother. After many years passed, Thebes began to suffer plagues and pestilence. To find out the reason for this affliction, Oedipus went to see Teiresias, a blind seer, who told Oedipus what happened between him and his parents. At first Oedipus would not believe the story but ultimately understood that it was true. His wife-queen and mother, Jocasta, committed suicide. Oedipus himself was so ashamed of his crimes that he tore out his eyes and sent himself into exile.

"Oedipus at Colonus," which Sophocles wrote the same year of his death, is about the exiled Oedipus. He wanders through the wilderness and tries to understand his crimes. His daughter, Antigone, takes care of him. Because he is blind, she leads him from place to place. She finds food and shelter for him. Because Oedipus is such an outcast, she must suffer his isolation with him. After he dies, she is free to return to Thebes.

The play, "Antigone," begins shortly after she returns home to Thebes, which is in a state of chaos and disorder. Eteocles and Polyneices – Oedipus's two sons – had been left in charge when their father sent himself into exit. The two brothers had agreed to share power and to alternate years of rule, but Eteocles refused to give up the throne after the first year. A war broke out between them, during which Polyneices and Eteocles killed each other. Polyneices's army fled and left their dead unburied. Their uncle, Creon, then became king.

During her exile with her father, Antigone developed a different set of values than most women of her age. She was independent and accustomed to making decisions. Being forced to return to a restricted life and taking orders from Creon was extremely difficult for her. Creon's situation was also challenging. He was taking over a city that was still divided. Allies of the two brothers continued to fight each other. Creon believed that his first task was to restore the city to order, which he did ruthlessly.

 "Antigone" is about more than the conflict between a rebellious girl, Antigone, and an iron-fisted ruler, Creon. Sophocles is writing about larger issues, including the conflict between an individual's conscience and the political and social need for order.

Read *Antigone* **online at:** http://classics.mit.edu/Sophocles/antigone.html.

Reading Hamlet

Most students today find Shakespeare's plays difficult to read. Given that the language he used has changed so much during the following 400 years, the challenge is easy to understand. If his works seem so difficult, the question is why do we continue to read and go see his plays? In a word: genius. Shakespeare is without peer as a playwright and poet. Once we see through the veil of his often difficult syntax and vocabulary, the nobility, inventiveness, and sheer magic of his works are self-evident.

In truth, it does get easier to read Shakespeare the more one reads him. Is it worth the effort? Certainly, not only on the basis of the works themselves, but also due to the vast literary endowment that Shakespeare left for generations of writers that followed. His influence is everywhere, even in our most contemporary writers.

Aside from practice reading, how else can you make the Bard of Stratford-upon-Avon more accessible? Read his works aloud. It is illuminating how reading his lines aloud makes them more understandable — and the poetry of his language more readily appreciated. Look also at the footnotes that are provided; they will explain words or passages you don't understand. A dictionary also helps, since some words' meanings have changed.

Shakespeare's Theatre

For many people who love Shakespeare's plays, the Bard and his works are closely associated with the Globe Theater. (To see a picture of Shakespeare's Globe Theater, go to http://www.greatbuildings.com/buildings/Globe_Theater.html.) Not all of his plays were performed at the Globe. He built it only after he had already become a successful playwright and did so to be able to use some of his theatrical innovations. In fact, the original theater was built for the Chamberlain's Men, William Shakespeare's company of players, in Bankside on the South side of the Thames in 1599.

Of course, many of Shakespeare's best known plays were performed in the Globe. For 14 years it was one of the most successful playhouses in London. Unfortunately, in 1613 a stage cannon set fire to the thatched roof of the building during a performance of "Henry VIII." The theatre burned to the ground. A second Globe was built on the same site. Scholars believe that Shakespeare may have acted in the second Globe, but he probably never wrote for it. Nevertheless, the Globe remained a home for Shakespeare's company until all theatres in England were forced to close by the Puritan government in 1642. Since it was no longer useful as a theater, the building was demolished to make room for housing for the poor.

What did the original Globe look like? We can't be positive because no construction drawings that show the original theatre exist today. Printed panoramas give us a rather basic idea of the exterior. Some written accounts, usually made by tourists, a building contract and one drawing of another nearby theater give us some idea about the interior. In addition, there are a few descriptive passages in the plays themselves, such as the famous Chorus at the opening of "Henry V": "And shall this cockpit hold within the vasty fields of France/Or may we cram within this wooden 'O'."

So what theatrical innovations did Shakespeare incorporate into his new theater? To make the Ghost in "Hamlet" more frightening to the audience, Shakespeare did not want him to just walk onstage. Instead, Shakespeare added a trap door in the floor of the stage. A platform under it could be slowly lifted to the level of the stage. The Ghost would wait on the platform, hidden from the audience. At the right time, the trap door would open and the platform would rise up. From the perspective of the audience, it would seem that the Ghost was arising through the floor of the stage. This innovative staging device became known as "the Hamlet Trap."

Theater-goers went to the Globe to see Shakespeare's plays during the day, since there were no electric lights and torches and lanterns were too dangerous. Fire was always a concern in those days. The audience was also seated in such a way that those in the gallery seats were mostly well-educated people who appreciated the subtleties in Shakespeare's plays. Those in the pit were less sophisticated and enjoyed more action, sex, and pratfalls in the plays. Cleverly, Shakespeare wrote his plays to appeal to both audiences. After each quiet scene or soliloquy, he would present a scene of great violence or comedy to keep his pit audience entertained.

Plot Summary of Hamlet

Hamlet is the son of Old Hamlet, the slain king of Denmark. Hamlet believes that his uncle, Claudius, has killed his father to gain the throne and marry his mother, Gertrude. Hamlet spends most of the play dressed in mourning for his dead father and attempting to elicit a confession from Claudius. He scolds his mother, Gertrude, for marrying Claudius too soon after her husband's death. She and Claudius are in the midst of celebrating their recent wedding.

Hamlet is in love with Ophelia, the daughter of Polonius and sister of Laertes. Laertes has advised Ophelia to ignore Hamlet until he is made king, at which point she should consent. Her father, Polonius, also forbids her to see Hamlet and she promises to obey his order.

The ghost that wanders the castle is the ghost of Old Hamlet. He confirms Hamlet's worst suspicions. The ghost tells the young Hamlet that he was sitting in the garden, asleep in his chair when Claudius came up to him and poured poison into his ear. He was killed immediately. The ghost of Old Hamlet then orders his son to seek revenge for this crime. Hamlet decides that he will pretend to be mad in order to fool Claudius and Gertrude until he is able to know if Claudius really killed his father. Polonius decides that Hamlet is mad because he told Ophelia to reject Hamlet's affections.

Hamlet decides to put on a play as a way of exposing his uncle's crime. The play is called The Mousetrap and involves a king who is murdered by his nephew while sleeping in the garden. Upon seeing the play, Claudius becomes outraged and leaves. This delights Hamlet, who is now convinced that the ghost was telling the truth. Meanwhile, Claudius is so overcome with emotion that he admits to killing his brother. Hamlet then goes to his mother's chambers. She becomes frightened by him and calls for help. Polonius, who is hiding behind a curtain in her room, makes a sound and Hamlet takes out a dagger and kills him through the curtain.

Ophelia goes mad at the death of her father. Laertes arrives from France and is intent on killing the murderer of his father. Claudius tells him that Hamlet is the murderer. Claudius plots a way to kill Hamlet by having Laertes fight him in a fencing match. Laertes decides to put poison on the tip of his sword so that any scratch will kill Hamlet. Claudius tells him he will also poison a cup of wine and give it to Hamlet as a backup measure. Gertrude then enters and tells the men that Ophelia has drowned herself in a brook.

Gertrude and Claudius go with Laertes to the graveside to bury Ophelia. They place her coffin into the ground and Laertes jumps into the grave in grief. Hamlet, when he realizes who is dead, comes out of hiding and also jumps into the grave. Laertes grabs Hamlet by the throat and Claudius orders the other men to separate them. Hamlet learns that Laertes has challenged him to a duel.

Laertes and Hamlet choose their foils and begin to fight. Hamlet scores a hit and Claudius drops a pearl into some wine, which he offers to Hamlet. Hamlet refuses to drink it. They fight again and Hamlet wins the next hit as well. Gertrude, delighted that Hamlet is winning, takes the cup of wine and drinks it to celebrate. Claudius suddenly realizes that she has drunk the poisoned wine, but he says nothing. The fight continues and Laertes slashes Hamlet with his poisoned lance. Hamlet attacks him, making Laertes drop the foil. Hamlet gets both rapiers and accidentally tosses his rapier over to Laertes. He then slashes Laertes with the poisoned foil.

They stop fighting when they realize that Gertrude is lying on the ground. Gertrude realizes that she has been poisoned and tells Hamlet that it was the drink. She dies, and Laertes tells Hamlet that he too is going to die from the poisoned tip. Hamlet slashes Claudius with the poisoned tip. He then takes the wine chalice and forces the poison into Claudius's mouth. Claudius dies and Laertes is also on the ground, dying. He forgives Hamlet for killing Polonius before he too dies. Hamlet tells the scholar, Horatio, that he must tell the people of Denmark what really happened and reveal the truth about his father's murder. Hamlet's final words are to make Fortinbras the next King of Denmark. Fortinbras orders his soldiers to give Hamlet a final military salute.

Issues in Hamlet

Most people familiar with the scope of Shakespeare's theatrical works would argue that "Hamlet" is one of his most complex. It is as much a play about the existential challenge of living in an imperfect world, as it is a story of betrayal and politics at the highest levels of society. More than anything, Hamlet is faced with moral, familial, and political challenges that he meets with courage and conviction.

One of the areas where scholars and critics have disagreed concerns Hamlet's relationship with Gertrude. Some argue that it seems incestuous; others suggest that Hamlet feels what any son would feel if his mother remarried so quickly after his father's death.

Another controversy concerns Gertrude herself: what does she know and when she did she know it? Does she know that Claudius killed Hamlet's father, her first husband? Was she in on it or was she a victim? What was Polonius' involvement in the plot to kill Old Hamlet? We know that he is a liar, but is he just being politically smart or is he, like Claudius, a criminal? Was Ophelia fragile and helpless or smart and more complex? Even her death raises questions: was it a suicide, an accident, or murder?

Of course, our greatest area of controversy concerns Hamlet himself. We know that he says he will pretend to be mad in order to discover the truth about his father. Given many of his other statements and actions, we might question how sane Hamlet really is. Under the circumstances – his father murdered by his uncle and his mother marrying the murderer – would some level of mental instability in Hamlet be all that extraordinary? Does he lose his mind? Is he evil? As with many great plays – and certainly with Shakespeare's – "Hamlet" leaves us with more questions than answers.

To read "Hamlet" go to: http://www.online-literature.com/shakespeare/hamlet/

Sample Test Questions

An important note about these test questions. Read before you begin. While all questions WILL test your knowledge, many will cover new areas that are not previously covered in this study guide. This is intentional. For questions that you do not answer correctly, take the time to study the question and the answer to prepare yourself for the test.

I. LITERATURE

A. READ ERNEST HEMINGWAY'S SHORT STORY "THE SHORT HAPPY LIFE OF FRANCIS MACOMBER" THEN CHOOSE THE BEST ANSWER TO THE FOLLOWING QUESTIONS:

1) Which of the following is the theme of this story?

    A) Hunting
    B) Deterioration of a marriage
    C) Adultery
    D) Murder
    E) Marriage

2) Which best describes the setting?

    A) African safari
    B) Emotional tension (between Macomber and Margot)
    C) Ego relations between a man and woman
    D) Hunting wild game
    E) All of the above

3) Which best describes the style of writing?

    A) Indirect
    B) Wordy, long-winded
    C) Highly economical
    D) Words flow slowly and lazily
    E) Victorian

4) What device does the author use primarily to reveal character?

    A) Long, detailed descriptions
    B) Their actions
    C) Their inner thoughts
    D) The clothes they wore
    E) Their dialogue

5) At what point does the climax occur in this story?

    A) When Macomber flees from the wounded lion
    B) When Margot shoots him
    C) When Margot goes to visit Wilson in his tent
    D) When Macomber "comes into his own" and finds courage in the excitement of the chase
    E) When Wilson treats him like a comrade

6) What is the denouement of the story? (The point at which all issues are resolved.)

    A) When Macomber "comes into his own" and finds courage in the excitement of the chase
    B) When Wilson accuses Margot of murder
    C) When Margot shoots Macomber
    D) When Wilson congratulates Macomber on finding his manhood
    E) When the two men hunt together

B. READ EDGAR ALLEN POE'S SHORT STORY "THE FALL OF THE HOUSE OF USHER," AND CHOOSE THE BEST ANSWER TO THE FOLLOWING QUESTIONS:

1) What does the house symbolize?

    A) Roderick, the current inhabitant
    B) The Usher family
    C) The illness of Roderick and his sister
    D) The narrator
    E) The area where it was located

2) Poe felt that the "tale" made possible the "fairest field for the exercise of the loftiest talent." He also wrote, "the unity of effect or impression is a point of the greatest importance." What "effect" or "impression" does this author strive for in this story?

A) Happy
B) Angry
C) Impending doom
D) Friendly
E) Scary

3) What is the *most important* means that the author uses to achieve this effect?

A) Descriptions
B) The history of the family
C) The reactions of the narrator
D) The supernatural happenings
E) The description of the house when the narrator arrives

4) What is the *most important* device that the author uses to reveal character?

A) Physical description
B) Their conversations
C) Statement by the narrator
D) Dialogue
E) Supernatural happenings

5) What is the point of view of this story?

A) Third person omniscient
B) Third person
C) Second person
D) First person narrator objective
E) First person narrator omniscient

6) What are the major conflicts in this story?

A) The narrator vs. the inhabitants of the house
B) Roderick vs. his sister
C) The Ushers vs. ultimate annihilation
D) The house vs. the inhabitants
E) The narrator vs. the house

7) By what specific devices is an identification between Roderick Usher and the house achieved?

    A) The personification of the house (eye-like windows, etc.)
    B) The description of the interior of the house
    C) The dialogue between him and the narrator
    D) The relationship between Roderick and his sister
    E) The poetry

C. READ HENRY JAMES' SHORT STORY "THE REAL THING" AND CHOOSE THE BEST ANSWER TO THE FOLLOWING:

1) Irony can be described as a discrepancy between what might reasonably be expected and what actually occurs—between the appearance of a situation and its reality. Where is there irony in this story by Henry James?

    A) The clothes the Monarchs wear compared to the clothes Miss Churm wears.
    B) The "sitters" doing housework.
    C) Miss Churm and Oronte posing as upper-class.
    D) The inability of the Monarchs to model upper-class figures.
    E) The discomfort of the narrator.

2) What is the major theme of this story?

    A) Upper class people sometimes lose their money.
    B) When upper-class people lose their money, they are helpless.
    C) Art is not a realistic picture of an object, but the creative representation of it.
    D) Lower-class people make good subjects for artists.
    E) Lower-class people do not respect upper-class people.

3) How does irony contribute to the theme (meaning) of the story?

    A) It makes the artist look more important.
    B) It doesn't contribute—it only makes the story more interesting.
    C) It shows the difference between the upper-class and lower-class.
    D) It presents a graphic picture of the nature of art.
    E) It makes the artist look incompetent.

4) What are the major conflicts in this story?

    A) They are internal—the artist struggles with the true nature of art.
    B) Upper-class vs. lower-class.
    C) Miss Churm vs. the Monarchs.
    D) Lower class people vs. the snobbery of the upper-class.
    E) Between the artist and the Monarchs.

5) How does James reveal character?

    A) Physical description
    B) The perception of the narrator
    C) Dialogue
    D) The setting of the studio
    E) The paintings

D) READ KATHERINE ANNE PORTER'S SHORT STORY "THEFT" FROM HER ANTHOLOGY FLOWERING JUDAS AND CHOOSE THE CORRECT ANSWER TO THE FOLLOWING QUESTIONS:

1) What are the conflicts in this story?

    A) The main character vs. a thieving universe.
    B) Camilo vs. Bill.
    C) The main character vs. Camilo.
    D) The main character vs. Bill.
    E) An interior one within the character.

2) What is the theme?

    A) An unwillingness to protect oneself is destructive.
    B) Servants will steal if they have a chance.
    C) Friends are not to be trusted.
    D) Women need protectors.
    E) You should always lock your doors.

3) What is the point of view?

    A) First person narrative.
    B) Third person narrative objective.
    C) Third person narrative omniscient.
    D) First person omniscient.
    E) Second person.

4) How does the character Camilo function in rendering the theme?

    A) He is careless about his new hat.
    B) In contrast to all the other people in her life, he is the only one who puts himself out to look after her rather than stealing from her.
    C) He is also poor.
    D) She rejects his efforts to help her.
    E) He is not attractive to her.

5) What is the climax of the action?

    A) When she finds her purse missing.
    B) When she determines to get her purse back and goes to find the janitress.
    C) When the janitress brings the purse back.
    D) When she gives the purse back to the janitress.
    E) When the janitress tries to humiliate her by refusing to take the purse.

6) What is the denouement (when all issues are resolved)?

    A) When the janitress refuses to take the purse.
    B) When the janitress refuses to take it and insults her.
    C) When she realizes that the thief is herself.
    D) When she remembers that she has never locked doors.
    E) When she goes to the basement to the basement to confront the janitress.

E. READ HAWTHORNE'S STORY "YOUNG GOODMAN BROWN" AND ANSWER THE FOLLOWING QUESTIONS:

1) Hawthorne often used allegory in his stories, and this story is almost entirely made up of allegory. An allegory is like a parable in that it tells a story that has a second meaning. Allegories don't necessarily always have a moral although parables usually do. What is the meaning of this allegory?

    A) Those who are proponents of high standards of behavior are usually hypocritical.
    B) Devil worship is bad.
    C) Devil worship is widespread.
    D) Husbands and wives should trust each other.
    E) Religion is not for everyone.

2) Hawthorne did not like the Transcendentalists of his day because he felt that their transparent optimism about the potentialities of human nature didn't match up with reality. How is that reflected in this story?

    A) Young Goodman Brown wasn't sure whether or not his visit to the forest was a dream.
    B) Faith continued to be a good wife.
    C) Young Goodman Brown snatches away a child that is being "catechized" by Goody Cloyse.
    D) He was so suspicious of everyone after his experience in the woods that his life and marriage were ruined.
    E) All the "good" people Young Goodman Brown knew had been involved in the evil meeting in the forest.

3) He gave the characters names that had a function in the story. How does the name Faith function in the story?

    A) Her husband is not sure whether or not she was at the evil ceremony in the woods.
    B) The family continued to pray, but he was an unwilling participant.
    C) When he pleaded with her not to participate, his "bad dream" ended.
    D) Before Young Goodman Brown went on his journey to the woods, just as faith is to a Christian, she was the center of his existence, but after his brush with evil, even she was not a comfort to him.
    E) We are not sure whether Faith was at the devil worshipping meeting.

4) This story is heavy in Biblical allusion and reference. What did the staff of the fellow traveler "which bore the likeness of a great black snake, so curiously wrought that it might almost be seen to twist and wriggle like a living serpent" signify?

    A) Evil
    B) The serpent in the Garden of Eve
    C) Aaron's rod
    D) The Devil
    E) All of the above

5) Hawthorne's life was overshadowed by the fact that his grandfather had been the "hanging judge" in the Salem witch trials. He carried a heavy burden of guilt as a result of his family heritage. How is that reflected in this story?

  A) Young Goodman Brown's guilt and suspicion ruled his life after the encounter in the woods.
  B) The "evil" in this story was the practice of witchcraft.
  C) The story is set in a small New England village.
  D) There is ambivalence about the "goodness" of the church members.
  E) All of the above.

II. POETRY

POEM #1

STOPPING BY WOODS ON A SNOWY EVENING
BY ROBERT FROST (1874-1963)

Whose woods are these I think I know.
His house is in the village though;
He will not see me stopping here
To watch his woods fill up with snow.

My little horse must think it queer
To stop without a farmhouse near
Between the woods and frozen lake
The darkest evening of the year.

He gives his harness bells a shake
To ask if there is some mistake.
The only other sound's the sweep
Of easy wind and downy flake.

The woods are lovely, dark and deep,
But I have promises to keep,
And miles to go before I sleep,
And miles to go before I sleep.

1) What is the "voice" or persona of this poem? (the speaker)

    A) A man burdened by his responsibilities
    B) A farmer
    C) A landowner
    D) A stranger
    E) A villager

2) What is his attitude?

    A) He is happy.
    B) He longs to stay in the woods.
    C) He is afraid of the owner of the woods.
    D) He is impatient with his horse.
    E) He is ambivalent.

3) What emotions is he expressing?

    A) Anger
    B) Longing
    C) Frustration
    D) Indifference
    E) Guilt

4) What is the theme?

    A) A ride on a snowy evening is refreshing.
    B) Taking advantage of the absence of the owner of the woods is gratifying.
    C) Responsibilities take precedence over pleasure.
    D) The beauty of nature.
    E) Animals are often impatient.

5) Many people who may not be able to recall the entire poem remember the last two lines. Why does he repeat the last line?

    A) He needed another line.
    B) It sounds good.
    C) It reinforces the theme.
    D) It leaves the image of life's responsibilities in the mind of the reader.
    E) It reminds the reader of the impatience of the horse.

6) What does the impatient horse symbolize?

    A) The urgencies of responsibility.
    B) The poet's wife.
    C) The owner of the woods.
    D) Nature.
    E) Animals respond to people's feelings.

7) This poem is written in perfect iambic tetrameter. How many feet are in each line?

    A) 5
    B) 4
    C) 6
    D) 3
    E) 2

8) Robert Frost's family had many problems such as depression and suicide, and he was responsible for looking after them. He was very successful as a famous poet, teacher and editor. What is there in this poem that reflects his life?

    A) His enjoyment of nature.
    B) The statement about the owner of the farm's not knowing he was there.
    C) The desire to escape his responsibilities.
    D) The snow in the woods.
    E) He gets tired.

POEM #2

A NARROW FELLOW IN THE GRASS
BY EMILY DICKENSON (1830-1886)

    A narrow fellow in the grass
    Occasionally rides;
    You may have met him—did you not?
    His notice sudden is.

    The grass divides as with a comb,
    A spotted shaft is seen;
    And then it closes at your feet
    And opens further on.

He likes a boggy acre,
A floor too cool for corn.
Yet when a boy, and barefoot,
I more than once, at morn.

Have passed, I thought, a whip lash
Unbraiding in the sun,–
When, stooping to secure it,
It wrinkled, and was gone.

Several of nature's people
I know, and they know me;
I feel for them a transport
Of cordiality;

But never met this fellow,
Attended or alone,
Without a tighter breathing,
and Zero at the Bone.

1) The persona of a poem is often not the poet, himself or herself. Who is the persona of this poem?

    A) An old woman
    B) A barefoot boy
    C) A man
    D) A young girl
    E) A mother

2) Who is this "narrow fellow in the grass"?

    A) A mouse
    B) A rabbit
    C) A groundhog
    D) A snake
    E) A porcupine

3) How does this poet feel about the "narrow fellow"?

    A) She likes him.
    B) She has no feeling about him.
    C) She is afraid of him.
    D) She avoids him.
    E) She is concerned for his welfare.

4) What is the theme of the poem?

   A) Some natural phenomena are intriguing but frightening.
   B) "Nature's people" should be protected.
   C) It's better to stay indoors.
   D) Animals like cool weather.
   E) Nature is beautiful.

5) A metaphor is an implied comparison. There are many metaphors in this poem. Pick the metaphor from the following list.

   A) Rides
   B) Narrow fellow
   C) Boggy acre
   D) Corn
   E) Grass divides

6) Pick the metaphor from this list.

   A) Whip lash
   B) Floor
   C) Tighter breathing
   D) Stooping
   E) Cordiality

7) Pick the metaphor from this list.

   A) Grass
   B) Zero at the Bone
   C) Notice
   D) Barefoot
   E) Morn

8) What image does "occasionally rides" suggest?

   A) Moves along quickly
   B) Is transported on a carriage or a train
   C) Climbs into the carriage from time to time
   D) Is sometimes picked up and carried
   E) Glides

9) The meter in this poem is not as regular as Frost's "Stopping by Woods. . ." What does the irregularity of rhythm do for the poem?

   A) Slows it down.
   B) Makes it harder to read.
   C) Reinforces the theme.
   D) Doesn't make any difference.
   E) Makes it rhythmic.

10) In the first stanza, the following pattern is found:

```
_ / _ / _ / _ /
_ / _ / _ /
_ / _ / _ – / _/
_ / _ /
```

   What is achieved by the break in the rhythm?

   A) It slows the reader down.
   B) It makes the verse seem conversational.
   C) It speeds the reader up.
   D) It doesn't make any difference.
   E) It makes it harder to read.

POEM #3

PIED BEAUTY
GERARD MANLEY HOPKINS (1844-1889)

   Glory be to God for dappled things—
      For skies of couple-colour as a brinded cow:
         For rose-moles all in stipple upon trout that swim;
   Fresh-firecoal chestnut-falls; finches' wings;
      Landscape plotted and pieced—fold, fallow, and plough;
         And all the trades, their gear and tackle and trim.

   All things counter, original, spare, strange;
      Whatever is fickle, freckled (who knows how?)
         With swift, slow; sweet, sour; adazzle, dim;
   He fathers-forth whose beauty is past change;
         Praise him.

Gerard Manley Hopkins was a Jesuit priest whose poetry was not recognized while he was alive. In fact, although he died in 1889, his works were not published until 1918 and only began to be recognized in 1930.

1) Who is the persona in this poem?

    A) A woman
    B) An old man
    C) A farmer
    D) The poet, himself, a priest
    E) A villager

2) Hopkins' philosophy emphasized the individuality of every natural thing, which he called "inscape." In the following items, select the one that *does not* reflect that philosophy.

    A) Whatever is fickle, freckled
    B) All the trades
    C) All things counter
    D) swift, slow; sweet, sour; adazzle, dim
    E) Praise him

3) He also initiated a new form of rhythm for his poetry, which he called "sprung" rhythm. It is measured by feet of from one to four syllables with any number of weak syllables. Contrary to the iambs (_/) of the poems by Frost and Dickenson, the stress is on the first syllable in "sprung" rhythm. The rhythm of the first two lines is as follows:

    /// _/_ / _/
    _/ /_ _/_ _/ /

In what way does this conform to the characteristics of "sprung" rhythm?

    A) It has iambs (_/).
    B) It has six feet.
    C) The first syllable is stressed.
    D) There are three stresses at the beginning.
    E) The second line begins with an unstressed syllable.

4) Hopkins' poetry is characterized by the strong images it suggests. What is a couple-colour sky?

    A) A blue sky.
    B) A cloudy sky.
    C) A stormy sky.
    D) A blue sky with many small bits of white clouds.
    E) A grey sky.

5) What does a brinded cow suggest?

    A) A Holstein.
    B) A black cow.
    C) A cow with a coat of two colors mixed together.
    D) A white cow.
    E) A brown cow.

6) What does "He fathers-forth whose beauty is past change" mean?

    A) His father is handsome.
    B) God is love.
    C) God makes all things.
    D) God's creation is diverse and it is beautiful.
    E) His father has beautiful children.

7) Alliteration is the repetition of a sound. Which of the following is an example of alliteration?

    A) Fathers-forth
    B) Beauty is past change
    C) Dappled things
    D) Brinded cow
    E) Beauty is past change

8) Select the example of alliteration from the following:

    A) Swift, slow; sweet, sour
    B) Chestnut-falls
    C) Finches' wings
    D) Counter, original, spare
    E) Rose-moles all in stipple

POEM #4

THE MAGI

WILLIAM BUTLER YEATS (1865-1939)

>Now as at all times I can see in the mind's eye,
>In their stiff, painted clothes, the pale unsatisfied ones
>Appear and disappear in the blue depth of the sky
>With all their ancient faces like rain-beaten stones,
>And all their helms of silver hovering side by side,
>And all their eyes still fixed, hoping to find once more,
>Being by Calvary's turbulence unsatisfied,
>The uncontrollable mystery on the bestial floor.

William Butler Yeats was an Irish poet who believed that prophesies had been revealed to him. He believed that the world goes in two-thousand-year cycles and that the Christian cycle would come to an end in the year 2000. He saw it as an ever-widening gyre with everything gradually coming apart and anarchy being loosed on the world. As the gyre widens, "things fall apart; the center cannot hold," he believed.

1) Where in "The Magi" is that theme found?

   A) I can see in the mind's eye
   B) The pale unsatisfied ones
   C) Helms of silver
   D) Being by Calvary's turbulence unsatisfied
   E) The blue depth of the sky

2) The rhythm in this poem is extremely irregular.
    The first two lines:
    / _ / _ _ / _ _ / _
    _ _ / / _ / _ / _/ _ _ /

    How does this very irregular rhythm enforce the theme?

   A) It is appropriate to a jarring theme.
   B) It doesn't enforce the theme.
   C) It provides a contrast to the theme of the Magi.
   D) It is not relevant to the theme.
   E) It makes the reading of it interesting.

3) What does the image of "Calvary's turbulence unsatisfied" suggest?

    A) That there will be another crucifixion.
    B) That the salvation bought by the crucifixion will no longer be sufficient.
    C) That there will be another virgin birth.
    D) That Calvary brought turbulence on the earth.
    E) That Christianity has brought unrest in the world.

4) What does "the pale unsatisfied ones" refer to?

    A) The three kings (the Magi) who brought gifts to the baby Jesus
    B) Christians who are no longer committed to their faith
    C) Non-Christians
    D) Devout Christians
    E) Leaders of the modern world

5) What does the bestial floor refer to?

    A) The anarchy to come
    B) People will behave like animals
    C) The birth of Jesus in a manger
    D) The widening gyre
    E) Conditions in the modern world

POEM #5

SONNET #60
WILLIAM SHAKESPEARE (1564-1616)

Like as the waves make toward the pebbled shore,
So do our minutes hasten to their end;
Each changing place with that which goes before,
In sequent toil all forwards do contend.
Nativity, once in the main (broad expanse) of light,
Crawls to maturity, wherewith being crowned,
Crooked eclipses 'gainst his glory fight,
And time that gave doth now his gift confound.
Time doth transfix the flourish (*remove the embellishment*) set on youth
And delves the parallels in beauty's brow,
Feeds on the rarities of nature's truth,
And nothing stands but for his scythe to mow.
And yet to times in hope (*future times*) my verse shall stand,
Praising thy worth, despite his cruel hand.

(Note: the italicized phrases in parentheses are translations of the phrase preceding.)

William Shakespeare is best known for his plays; however, he wrote a number of sonnets like #60. They were not published in his lifetime. It appears that he wrote them for his friends and not for publication.

1) What is the theme of Sonnet #60?

    A) Passage of time.
    B) The effects of the passage of time on a human being.
    C) Poems will endure even after the poet is dead.
    D) Time is the enemy of youth.
    E) Growing old is depressing.

2) Who is the persona?

    A) A lover who is growing older
    B) An old man
    C) A young man
    D) A woman
    E) A young lover

3) To whom is he/she speaking?

    A) No one in particular
    B) A lover who is growing older
    C) His/her children
    D) His/her friends
    E) His family

4) What simile (direct comparison) can you find in this sonnet?

    A) "Like as the waves make towards the pebbled shore, so do our minutes hasten to their end"
    B) "In sequent toil all forwards do contend"
    C) "And time that gave doth now his gift confound"
    D) "And yet to times in hope my verse shall stand"
    E) "Feeds on the rarities of nature's truth"

5) What metaphor (implied comparison) can you find?

    A) "In sequent toil all forwards do contend"
    B) "And nothing stands but for his scythe to mow"
    C) "Time doth transfix the flourish set on youth"
    D) "Each changing place with that which goes before"
    E) "In sequent toil all forwards do contend"

6) The rhythm is a consistent iambic pentameter (5 feet of iambs– _ /). However, there are two lines where this rhythm is broken. In the following, what is the line where the rhythm is not iambic pentameter?

    A) Line 1
    B) Line 13
    C) Line 6
    D) Line 7
    E) Line 2

III. DRAMA

A. GREEK DRAMA

1) Who wrote *Antigone*?

    A) Euripides
    B) Sophocles
    C) Aristophanes
    D) Tantalus
    E) Polyneices

2) Sophocles' tragedies always present a titanic heroic figure defiantly refusing to compromise and bend to other people's different perception of reality. Who is that figure in *Antigone*?

    A) Antigone, herself
    B) Kreon
    C) Ismene
    D) Haimon
    E) Jason

3) What is the conflict in *Antigone*?

    A) Antigone vs. Creon
    B) Political—supporter of one brother over supporter of another
    C) Moral—right vs. wrong
    D) Family—sister vs. uncle
    E) Ego—Creon uses force to get his way

4) What is the theme of *Antigone*?

    A) Rulers are obligated to behave ethically.
    B) Rulers are entitled to take sides in political issues.
    C) Blood is thicker than water.
    D) It is heroic to take a stand for one's beliefs.
    E) How a person is buried is important.

5) Who was Antigone's father?

    A) Creon
    B) Oedipus
    C) Polyneices
    D) Kapaneus
    E) Tiresius

B. SHAKESPEARE'S PLAYS

A Midsummer Night's Dream

1) Shakespeare often uses a device called dramatic irony: when a speaker's words convey to his listeners a meaning that he does not comprehend, since they are aware of facts of which he is ignorant, creating a double meaning. In *A Midsummer Night's Dream*, dramatic irony is used often. Which of the following demonstrates dramatic irony in this play?

    A) Bottom's ignorance of his ass's head.
    B) Theseus rejecting the story the lovers tell him.
    C) Quince assigning the parts to the players.
    D) Tom Snout accepting his part without comment.
    E) Hippolyta's nonchalance about her upcoming marriage.

2) Shakespeare also often uses contrast skillfully in his plays. Where in this play does he demonstrate this skill?

    A) Bottom (which means a skein of yarn), whose name suggests his profession (weaver).
    B) Robin Starveling, the tailor playing the part of Thisbe's mother.
    C) Helena's pursuit of Demetrius.
    D) Daintiness and immateriality in the fairies and the crudeness and materialism of the clowns.
    E) Lysander and Demetrius.

3) A *masque* is a drama combining music and dancing with lyric poetry and a theme calling for magnificence of display. Which of the following demonstrates how *A Midsummer Night's Dream* fits that definition?

    A) The characters are noble.
    B) The theme is a wedding; and music, dancing and lyrics are found in most of the chief scenes.
    C) It is about upper-class young people and their love life.
    D) It has fairies as major characters.
    E) It starts with a scene in the palace.

Act II, scene I—Titania's long speech

> Therefore the winds, piping to us in vain,
> As in revenge, have suck'd up from the sea
> Contagious fogs; which, falling in the land,
> Hath every pelting river made so proud
> 5   That they have overborne their continents:
> The ox hath therefore stretch'd his yoke in vain,
> The ploughman lost his sweat, and the green corn
> Hath rotted ere his youth attain'd a beard;
> The fold stand empty in the drowned field,
> 10   And crows are fatted with the murrion flock;
>
> The human mortals want their winter here;
> No night is now with hymn or carol blest:
> Therefore the moon, the governess of floods,
> Pale in her anger, washes all the air,
> 15   That rheumatic diseases do abound:
> And through his distemperature we see
> The seasons alter: hoary-headed frosts
> Fall in the fresh lap of the crimson rose,
> And on old Hiem's thin and icy crown
> An odorous chaplet of sweet summer buds
> Is, as in mockery, set.

4) Personification—giving human characteristics to a non-human item—is used often by Shakespeare. From the following list, choose the item that is an example of personification.

    A) ". . .Contagious fogs; which, falling in the land."
    B) "The human mortals want their winter here;"
    C) The reference to the green corn as a youth as yet without a beard.
    D) "An odorous chaplet of sweet summer buds"
    E) "The human mortals want their winter here;"

5) Metaphor—an implied comparison—is another figure of speech often used by Shakespeare. Of the following, which is an example of a metaphor?

    A) "drowned field" for a flooded field
    B) "An odorous chaplet of sweet summer buds"
    C) "No night is now with hymn or carol blest:"
    D) "The seasons alter:"
    E) "The ox hath therefore stretch'd his yoke in vain"

6) As with other poets, Shakespeare makes use of alliteration—the repetition of sounds—in his poetry. Which of the following is an example of alliteration in the above lines?

   A) "Pale in her anger, washes all the air."
   B) "And on old Hiem's thin and icy crown."
   C) "No night is now with hymn or carol blest:"
   D) "Therefore the moon, the governess of floods."
   E) "The ploughman lost his sweat,"

7) Shakespeare often uses rustic elements in his plays. What is one instance of this in this play?

   A) Court life in the opening scene.
   B) The relationship between Lysander and Hermia at the beginning of the play.
   C) Act V, Scene I, in the palace.
   D) A wood peopled at midnight with fairies, lovers, artisans, and wild animals.
   E) The conflict between father and daughter over her choice of husband.

8) What is the connection of the following passage with the theme of the play? "The course of true love never did run smooth."

   A) It is the theme of the play.
   B) It is about Demetrius and Helena.
   C) It is about the fairies.
   D) It is about Bottom.
   E) It is about the marriage of Theseus and Hippolyta.

9) There are three "worlds" in this play. What are they?

   A) The world of Demetrius; the world of Hermia; and the world of Lysander.
   B) The world of the father demanding that his daughter marry a man she doesn't love; the world of the Athenian workmen; and the world of the fairies.
   C) The world of Oberson; the world of Titania; and the world of Puck.
   D) The world of Bottom; the world of Quince; and the world of Flute.
   E) The world of the court; the world of the play; and the world in the woods.

10) In *Midsummer's Night's Dream,* what is Puck's real name?

A) Lysander
B) Robin Goodfellow
C) Theseus
D) Demetrius
E) Robin Hood

Other Plays by Shakespeare

1) In *King Lear*, which of the king's three daughters is a sympathetic character?

A) Cordelia
B) Goneril
C) Regan
D) Elizabeth
E) Ann

2) In *Othello,* why is Iago so angry at Othello that he sets out to destroy him?

A) He resented him because he was black.
B) He didn't want to leave Venice.
C) He was in love with Desdemona.
D) He thought Othello was having an affair with his wife, Emilia.
E) Othello passed him over for Cassio for the position of chief lieutenant.

3) Many famous phrases have come into common uses from Shakespeare's plays. What play does the phrase: "loved not wisely but too well" come from?

A) *Measure for Measure*
B) *A Midsummer Night's Dream*
C) *Romeo and Juliet*
D) *Othello*
E) *Much Ado About Nothing*

4) In *Romeo and Juliet,* who is the girl that Romeo goes looking for when he finds Juliet instead?

A) Annette
B) Elizabeth
C) Rosalind
D) Regan
E) Maria

5) What genre is *Julius Caesar?*

   A) Comedy
   B) History
   C) Miracle
   D) Masque
   E) Tragedy

C. MODERN DRAMA

Eugene O'Neill's *Desire Under the Elms*

1) *Desire Under the Elms* is called a naturalistic tragedy; that is, it represents the endeavor of the modern world to express the tragic implications of its characteristic outlook on life. How does it demonstrate this genre?

   A) The setting of a drab, rundown farmhouse in New England in 1850
   B) The characters who live their lives out in desperation
   C) The plot—everything comes undone
   D) The protagonist whose outlook is bleak
   E) All of the above

2) What is the theme?

   A) Families are difficult to live with.
   B) The whole concept of family is destructive.
   C) Life is hard.
   D) Belief in God can become a destructive force.
   E) Lust is a dominating force in human beings.

3) Which character is most responsible for the tragedy?

   A) Eben
   B) Abbie
   C) Simeon
   D) Ephraim
   E) Peter

4) While we may feel that what we are seeing on the stage is real, it is the nature of the art of drama to present an illusion of reality. In other words, our rational minds may tell us that a thing might not be expected to happen in the real world, we are, nevertheless, able to participate as observers in that thing. What, in this play, is something that we might not accept rationally, yet are able to be moved by artistically?

    A) The characters are overdrawn, yet they have some characteristics that we have known in the people we know or observe.
    B) The plot is extreme, but we know that sometimes stepmothers do become involved with their stepsons.
    C) While greed plays a more extreme role in this play that we expect in real life, nevertheless, greed is a part of everyone's life.
    D) The killing of the baby in the heat of an emotional moment is extreme, yet we know that anguished mothers do sometimes kill their children.
    E) All of the above.

5) The setting in this story can almost be said to be a character in the story. What role does this "character" play in the story?

    A) The hardness and the intractability of the farm is directly reflected in the protagonist.
    B) Its beauty provides a contrast to its stubborn intractability, which reflects what Ephraim calls "softness" in Eben and his mother.
    C) The farm has yielded a meager subsistence, which symbolizes a family that has yielded twisted, spiritually impoverished offspring.
    D) The sheriff closes the play thus: "It's a jim-dandy farm, no denyin'. Wished I owned it!" The entire play was about the ownership of a farm that destroyed the people who owned it, so the farm itself carried the theme of the play.
    E) All of the above.

IV. LITERARY TERMS

1) Which term indicates the main character?

    A) Round character
    B) Antagonist
    C) Minor character
    D) Protagonist
    E) Flat character

2) Which of the following terms indicates the adversary or opponent of the main character?

    A) Antagonist
    B) Protagonist
    C) Flat character
    D) Round character
    E) Major Character

3) In early Greek drama, the hero was always noble. There were no lower-class protagonists. However, in modern times, the character in this role has sometimes been less than heroic. Which of the following terms designates this kind of protagonist?

    A) Dynamic character
    B) Static character
    C) Anti-hero
    D) Antagonist
    E) Flat Character

4) Sometimes a story is about the evolution of a character. He/she may attain self-knowledge and become a different character, or something may happen to that character in the course of the story that has the impact of bringing about a change. An unsympathetic character may become more sympathetic. A weak character may become strong. Which of the following terms designates this kind of character?

    A) Round character
    B) Flat character
    C) Minor character
    D) Static character
    E) Dynamic character

5) We see limited sides of some characters in a story or a play. They may be in the work only to advance the action, or a skimpily developed character may provide a contrast to the protagonist, who is usually more fully developed. What term is used to designate the character that is not very well developed?

    A) Anti-hero
    B) Static character
    C) Flat character
    D) Round character
    E) Antagonist

6) Not all characters are fully developed for reasons of economy and utility. The action of a play or a story may be slowed down by having too many characters that we get to know in too much depth. This can become tedious and tiring. However, the story will not engage unless there is adequate development of some of the characters. These fully-developed or semi fully developed characters are characterized by what term?

   A) Round character
   B) Flat character
   C) Antagonist
   D) Static character
   E) Anti-hero

7) Just as a story may turn on the changes that are taking place in a character, so a story may be about a character that does not change even in the light of what might be considered life-changing occurrences. What is the character called who does not change?

   A) Round character
   B) Flat character
   C) Static character
   D) Anti-hero
   E) Dynamic character

8) Point of view is a very powerful tool used by writers to control the way a reader will react to a story. The point of view chosen will determine whether the reader is in the minds of all the characters, some of the characters, or none of the characters. If the story is being told by a person who was a participant and is telling the story, what term is used to designate the point of view?

   A) Second person
   B) First person narrator
   C) Third person
   D) Third person narrator
   E) Third person omniscient narrator

9) If an observer is telling the story, the thoughts of those being observed may or may not be revealed. What is the term that designates an observer narrator who is able to report what all the characters are thinking?

    A) First person narrator
    B) Third person narrator
    C) Third person narrator omniscient
    D) First person omniscient
    E) Unreliable narrator

10) The phrase "gray-eyed Athena" is an example of

    A) Epithet
    B) Onomatopoeia
    C) Rectitude
    D) Allegory
    E) None of the above

11) If the character is morally scrupulous they may be considered to have

    A) Epithet
    B) Onomatopoeia
    C) Rectitude
    D) Allegory
    E) Personification

12) Myth, illusion and untruth are synonyms for

    A) Fallacy
    B) Onomatopoeia
    C) Rectitude
    D) Allegory
    E) Personification

13) The phrase "Little strokes/Fell great oaks" is an example of

    A) Fallacy
    B) Epigram
    C) Rectitude
    D) Epithet
    E) Personification

Answer Key

I. Literature

A. "The Short Happy Life
    of Francis Macomber"
1) B
2) C
3) C
4) B
5) D
6) C

B. "The Fall of the House of Usher
1) B
2) C
3) E
4) C
5) E
6) C
7) A

C. "The Real Thing"
1) D
2) C
3) D
4) A
5) A
6) E
7) A

D. "Theft"
1) E
2) A
3) A
4) B
5) B
6) C

E. "Young Goodman Brown"
1) A
2) E
3) D
4) E
5) E

II. POETRY

Poem #1
1) A
2) B
3) B
4) C
5) C
6) A
7) B
8) C

Poem #2
1) C
2) D
3) C
4) A
5) A
6) A
7) B
8) B
9) C
10) B

Poem #3
1) D
2) E
3) C
4) D
5) C
6) D
7) A
8) A

Poem #4
1) D
2) A
3) B
4) A
5) C

Poem #5
1) B
2) A
3) B
4) A
5) B
6) C

III. DRAMA

A. Greek Drama
1) B
2) A
3) C
4) D
5) B

B. Shakespeare Plays
Midsummer Night's Dream
1) A
2) D
3) B
4) C
5) A
6) C
7) D
8) A
9) B
10) B

Other Plays
1) A
2) E
3) D
4) C
5) E

C. Modern Drama
Desire Under the Elms
1) E
2) D
3) B
4) E
5) E

IV. LITERARY TERMS

1) D
2) A
3) C
4) E
5) C
6) A
7) C
8) B
9) C
10) A
11) C
12) A
13) B

Test Taking Strategies

Here are some test-taking strategies that are specific to this test and to other CLEP tests in general:

- Keep your eyes on the time. Pay attention to how much time you have left.
- Read the entire question and read all the answers. Many questions are not as hard to answer as they may seem. Sometimes, a difficult sounding question really only is asking you how to read an accompanying chart. Chart and graph questions are on most CLEP tests and should be an easy free point.
- If you don't know the answer immediately, the new computer-based testing lets you mark questions and come back to them later if you have time.
- Read the wording carefully. Some words can give you hints to the right answer. There are no exceptions to an answer when there are words in the question such as "always" "all" or "none." If one of the answer choices includes most or some of the right answers, but not all, then that is not the answer. Here is an example:

    The primary colors include all of the following:
    A) Red, Yellow, Blue, Green
    B) Red, Green, Yellow
    C) Red, Orange, Yellow
    D) Red, Yellow, Blue
    E) None of the above

    Although item A includes all the right answers, it also includes an incorrect answer, making it incorrect. If you didn't read it carefully, were in a hurry, or didn't know the material well, you might fall for this.
- Make a guess on a question that you do not know the answer to. There is no enalty for an incorrect answer. Eliminate the answer choices that you know are incorrect. For example, this will let your guess be a 1 in 3 chance instead.

 # *What Your Score Means*

Based on your score, you may, or may not, qualify for credit at your specific institution. At University of Phoenix, a score of 50 is passing for full credit. At Utah Valley State College, the score is unpublished, the school will accept credit on a case-by-case basis. Another school, Brigham Young University (BYU) does not accept CLEP credit. To find out what score you need for credit, you need to get that information from your school's website or academic advisor.

You can score between 20 and 80 on any CLEP test. Some exams include percentile ranks. Each correct answer is worth one point. You lose no points for unanswered or incorrect questions.

 # Test Preparation

How much you need to study depends on your knowledge of a subject area. If you are interested in literature, took it in school, or enjoy reading then your studying and preparation for the literature or humanities test will not need to be as intensive as someone who is new to literature.

This book is much different than the regular CLEP study guides. This book actually teaches you the information that you need to know to pass the test. If you are particularly interested in an area, or you want more information, do a quick search online. We've tried not to include too much depth in areas that are not as essential on the test. Everything in this book will be on the test. It is important to understand all major theories and concepts listed in the table of contents. It is also very important to know any bolded words.

Don't worry if you do not understand or know a lot about the area. With minimal study, you can complete and pass the test.

 # Legal Note

FLASHCARDS

This section contains flashcards for you to use to further your understanding of the material and test yourself on important concepts, names or dates. You can cut these out to study from or keep them in the study guide, flipping the page over to check yourself.

Theme

Plot

Fiction

Tale

Short Story

Parable

Allegory

Fable

Events that take place in the story

Central idea of the story

A story

A created story, no real characters

Short moral story

A fictional story, usually a narrative

A brief story that points to a moral, animals with current traits

Story where abstract ideas are represented

Initiation Story

In Medias Res

Flash Back

Main Character

Protagonist

Antagonist

Setting

Epiphany

When a story starts in the middle of an action

Where a character goes through rites of initiation

The primary character in a story

When the story goes back in time

The adversary or opponent

Another name for main character

When a character has a sudden realization

Time, location or place where a story takes place

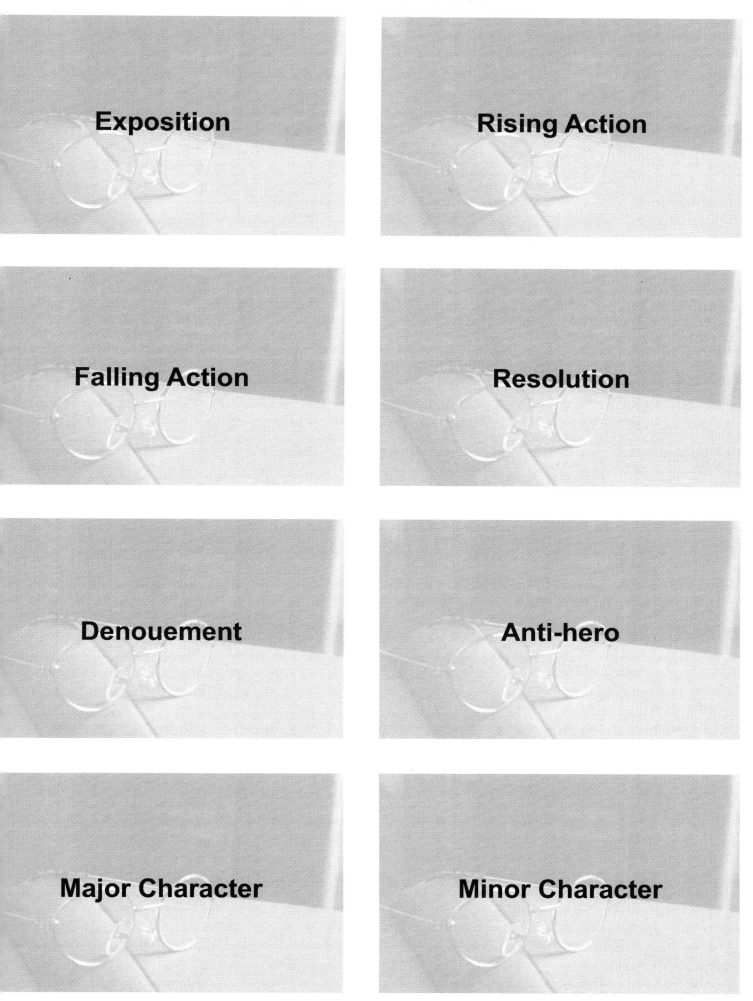

Exposition

Rising Action

Falling Action

Resolution

Denouement

Anti-hero

Major Character

Minor Character

Where the reader finds out about the conflict and includes new problems

Where the reader meets the characters and settings

What happens after the climax

What happens after the climax

A protagonist that doesn't have the noble characteristics that would make him a hero

What happens after the climax

A supporting character

A character the story is focused on

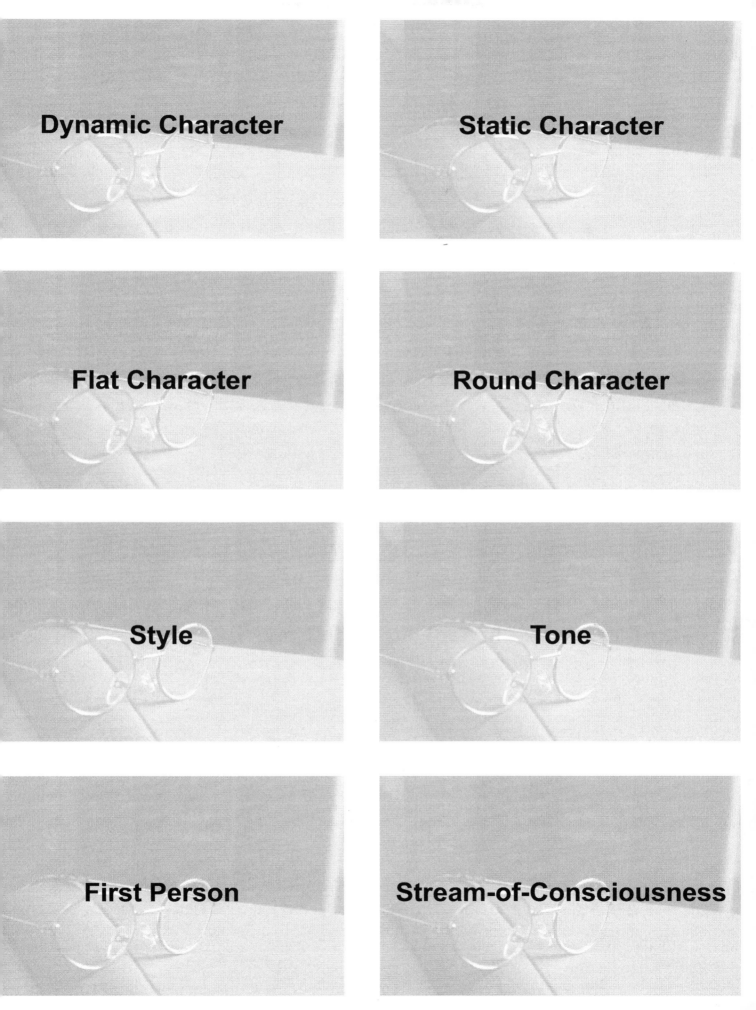

Dynamic Character

Static Character

Flat Character

Round Character

Style

Tone

First Person

Stream-of-Consciousness

A stable character that does not change during the story

A character that changes during the story

A fully developed character with good and bad things about them

Not a very developed character-only has one or tw traits

The mood of a subject

The way a story was writter shows the author's flair and touch

An unedited view of the speaker's mind

Where the speaker talks about himself or herself

Narrator

Naïve Narrator

Third Person Narrator

Third Person Objective Narrator

Third Person Limited Narrator

Third Person Omniscient Narrator

Unreliable Narrator

Point of View

A narrator that doesn't understand the conflicts about the story he is telling

The person who tells the stor

This narrator can't tell the reader the thoughts of the characters

A narrator that is not a participant in the story

The narrator is all knowing

Narrator knows only about one character

The way a story is told and by whom

A narrator that is mentally unstable

Symbol	Allegory
Voice	**Persona**
Word Order	**Imagery**
Figure of Speech	**Simile**

A story with two levels of meaning, literal and symbolic

A thing that suggests more than its literal meaning

The person who tells the story

Speaker in a poem

Language that evokes one of the five senses

The way words are arranged in the poem

Comparison between two different items, using "like" or "as"

Describes one thing in terms of something else

Metaphor

Personification

Climax

Subplot

Monologue

Soliloquy

Scenery

Props

Giving human characteristics to inanimate objects

Comparison between two different items, NOT using "like" or "as"

A less important plot, developed at the same time

Where the tension of the plot is at its height

Speech toward the audience

Extended speech by one character

Items on the set

The setting on the stage, houses, a room, etc.